The Sensational Liquid
A guide to wine tasting

by Malcolm Gluck

Friend or foe? A cork can cosset or it can kill a wine.

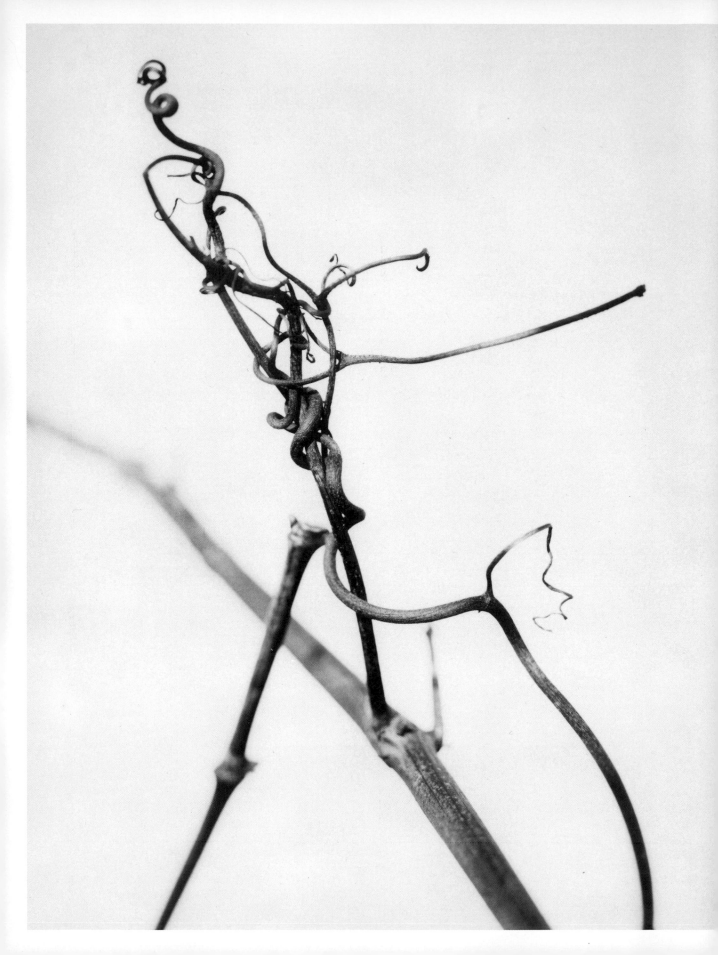

The Sensational Liquid
A guide to wine tasting

by Malcolm Gluck

Photography by Robin Grierson

Hodder & Stoughton

Is this the beginning of a wonderful journey?

First published in Great Britain in 1999 by Hodder and Stoughton
A division of Hodder Headline PLC

10 9 8 7 6 5 4 3 2 1

A CIP catalogue record for this title is available from the British Library

ISBN 0 340 71310 0

Printed and bound in Great Britain by
The Bath Press

Hodder and Stoughton
A division of Hodder Headline PLC
338 Euston Road
London NW1 3BH

To Madame de Gaillac
for introducing me, on the evening
of the 29 May 1964,
to every sensation wine can evoke.

Contents

Introduction: The Five Senses

You may have them all,
but do you also possess the nerve?
Page 16

A Debt Acknowledged

It is not possible to raise and bake a volume like this without the author having more than his own pair of hands to knead the dough. In developing and writing this book I am indebted to a good many individuals who were helpful and I thank them though I recognize that any errors must be mine not theirs.

Bill Blatch at Vintex must head the list of people whose input was crucial for he wrote such a remarkable vineyard report I felt it it imperative it was included herein in its entirety.

For giving me their time and providing illuminating insight, I thank **Geoffrey Taylor** at Corkwise, **Pierre-Yves Bournerias** of the Institut Oenologique de Champagne, **Agnes Dezsenyi, Stefano Girelli,** loads of people at **Fetzer Vineyards** (**Phil Hurst** was especially illuminating) **Michael Goundrey, Nick Butler, Guy Anderson, Nigel Sneyd**, and **Nerida Abbott**. I would particularly like to thank **Gaetane Carron** for lending me an instructive book and **Ann Noble** at Davies University for lending me a sympathetic ear (one warm afternoon in California). I thank **Nicola Daubney** at the Wine and Spirit Education Trust, **Victoria Morrall** for an interesting piece of paper, **Michael Paul** and **Richard Gibson** at Penfold's, and **Lindsay Talas** and **Nicky Walden** of Tesco.

I must express my gratitude to **Paul Bramfitt** at John Jenkins & Co. and **Verity Matthews** (who tolerated snapshot anarchy at Photo Me International Plc). **Sune Van Zyl** of Wines of South Africa was a dream (as was **Rosamund Hitchcock** of R & R Teamwork). **Riette Steyn** of the South Africa Wine and Spirit Exporters Association were hugely helpful and I thank both of them as well as thanking **Allan Nelson** of Nelson's Creek and all the people from New Beginnings in the Cape.

I would particularly like to kneel in appreciation of the efforts of my two editors, **Susan Hill** and **Rowena Webb**, who between them stretched the author and made his book a tauter piece of work. I acknowledge also **Laura Brockbank**'s patience. I am grateful to **Nachtmann UK** who supplied the glasses and **Annabel Alford** at Saffron PR who helped here.

I owe a big debt to **Robin Grierson** who, often in fraught conditions, photographed everything so forcefully and unpretentiously and I know he would like to thank **Kodak** for help with film stock.

I thank **Caroline Park** at the **Australian Wine Commission** and all those at the **Cafe Royal's Australian Wine tasting event** who didn't object to the intrusion, however discreetly, of Robin's lens. For the beguiling portraits of themselves in this book, I thank the beautiful **Rachel Weisz** and **Neil Morrissey, Julian** and **Paul Vogel, Lee Bollam, Pietro Ferri** and **Lord Eatwell** of Queens' College Cambridge, **Frank Usher, Glory, Teddy, Oscar, Pauline** and **Howard Romps**. Thank you **Emma Pocock** at Berry Brothers & Rudd, thank you, **Lamberhurst Wines Ltd**, and thanks very much, **Joseph the govnor** at the delicious BYOB **Mandola Café** in Westbourne Grove. Thanks are also due to **Sue Allatt, Ben, Scarlet, Ruby & Amber Evans, Lottie, Daisy** and **Rebecca Grierson Romp**.

Lastly, I would like to acknowledge, from the bottom of my ink horn, the tremendous creative debt this book owes to **Suzi Godson**, **Mel Agace** and **Junko Fuwa** at UNLIMITED whose commitment to the art direction and design of this book made collaborating with them such a rich pleasure.

Cheers, everyone.

Please be seated at Berry Brothers & Rudd, Mayfair.

The wines push themselves at Tesco.

Introduction: The Five Senses

(You may have them all, but do you also possess the nerve?)

At table, my children laugh at me. They apologize for their father to their friends. My wife's acquaintances balance their raised eyebrows with barely upturned lips: polite smiles. A girlfriend, years ago now, who repeatedly refused to marry me, would ostentatiously flourish a set of earplugs whenever wine was poured for me to taste. I've noticed luncheon companions regard me pityingly. 'Poor chap,' their expressions say. 'I wonder if he's tried counselling?'

I understand. I know how they feel. But I just can't help myself. I have to taste wine properly.

Yet when I first witnessed the theatricality of wine tasting I too could barely suppress a snort of disdain. It was in the spring of the year England ran off with the soccer World Cup. I'd been drinking wine for two years. And then someone who really knew what he was doing invited me to share a bottle of my first real wine experience, Château Margaux 1947. This cabernet sauvignon, cabernet franc and merlot get-together cost 75 shillings and sixpence at a pub with an upstairs wine bar — one of only four in London at that time — in Marylebone's Thayer Street . (Such a bordeaux in decent condition today might fetch £750, it might go for £1000. Certainly you should get away with paying less than the £2500 a bottle at which Château Cheval Blanc of the same vintage is valued. That's the current price of a single bottle of Cheval Blanc '47 at one London wine merchant and this great St-Emilion was also one of my early, affordable experiences in those heady far-off days of the mid-sixties. A whole case of this cabernet franc/merlot marriage today? £37,400 was the quoted price at one London merchant — one of the few to have 12 bottles — last time I looked.)

What a pretentious berk I thought this person as he smelled the cork. Why would he do that? More grotesque theatre was to follow. I simply took a gulp of the wine and thought nothing more than how much richer it was than any wine I'd had before. But my generous companion was sniffing at it — so little in his huge glass! — and sniffing again and again while an expression, which I can only compare to my own when I first heard, disappointed in love, the third movement of Tchaikovsky's 'Pathétique', gripped his features, he sighed, gargled with the blessed wine, rinsed his teeth in the stuff and then, after what seemed an absurd length of time, he permitted the wine, finally, after several curtain calls, to quit the stage and descend his throat.

I tried to look away. I fidgeted. I had another gulp from my glass (which was, now that I noticed it, huge also). I felt embarrassed. I hoped the other customers wouldn't think my companion sufficiently eccentric or threatening to feel it necessary to summon the men in white coats.

Yet within five minutes I was doing exactly what he had done. There was, it was demonstrably clear to me, no other way fully to appreciate what was in my glass. Later, all I could feel was that I had wasted two years on wine drinking which should have been spent wine tasting. I felt as stupid, and as wonderfully liberated and empowered, as if I'd spent the past two years, in blissful, semi-deaf ignorance, listening to music with earplugs in place which had now, suddenly, been removed. I was enjoying the experience in a fresh and invigorating way.

You have, then, been warned. You may have the nose for it. You may have the palate. You may possess the all-consuming appetite for tasting wine. But if you lack the stomach to make a fool of yourself, in public, you should stick to sipping. You won't offend anyone. No one'll call the cops. You won't have the neighbours giving you a wide berth in the street.

You won't of course ever understand wine and you won't die with a beatific grin on your mug. But you'll never have to worry about little red dribbles staining the front of your blouse/shirt, trousers/skirt.

Live your life with your head in a paperbag, why don't you?

A drinking glass, not a tasting glass.

To the professional wine taster, the wine glass is a tool.

1 The First Lesson

(Or tasting wine at the right speed)

No clever-clogs expert knows what you know about wine. For only you know what you like. And nobody can tell you you're wrong. What is wine if it is not about personal enjoyment? Without enjoyment, pure pleasure, wine is a barren irrelevance. Wine, then, is not about a struggle to stuff yourself full of arcane knowledge of dubious value. However, the more wine you drink, the more curious you become about it. Hence my hope that this book will find fertile and curious minds to pore over it as diligently as they pour the liquid it celebrates.

Let me say, first, that there has never been a book quite like this before. To be sure, others have offered tasting texts, scientific, professional, perhaps a touch starchy, on the smelling, gargling and spitting out of wine, and there are general guides to wine. But in these pages I am attempting to go into the subject, hopefully in an entertaining yet authoritative way, and answer all the questions, cover all the latest research, delve into the myriad factors affecting the enjoyment of the taste of wine which have never before been tackled in such depth and with such approachability. I hope, in this way, to offer both the straightforward wine lover and the highly experienced imbiber (not to mention professional wine buyers and wine makers who should find something to detain them here) a useful fund of knowledge.

Second, why me? I am a wine correspondent and wine-guide compiler, wine lover and occasional cook, who has spent well over thirty years fascinated by wine, its talismanic place in human relationships, and its marriage with food. I can claim no scientific qualifications to write this book. However, I am a writer who relishes the challenge (a daily one) of putting into words what is basically ineffable. I am committed to giving my readers the pleasure of both a well-honed sentence and a handsomely tuned wine. I am enemy to the pretension which bedevils the world of wine and creates barriers to enjoyment. And I am acutely conscious of the many factors which prevent drinkers enjoying wine in perfect condition.

Third, I feel driven to write a book which will give its readers a surer grasp of the glass and the liquid within it and empower them both to enjoy wine all the more and to recognize that it is not the hoity-toity and messily complicated subject many self-serving experts make it out to be. This book is a guide to how to enjoy yourself drinking wine.

It is not strictly a book which begins at Chapter 1 and ends at Chapter 18. You can dip in and out as you please, at the pace which coincides with your interest and your level of expertise, or suits your temperament. There is a chapter which is straightforwardly How to Taste and more complex chapters which are based on extensive study and research into scientific and technical aspects of wine which have a direct bearing on the subject of its taste and its appreciation. Valuable knowledge, I sincerely trust, is to be found on every page.

I do not expect to turn my readers, my wine-loving readers, into hyper-sensitive critics or touchy cynics. Many a critic has a sullen disposition which only turns cheery when a fault is found. A lover of the subject is more inclined to nose about for routes to enjoyment. Therefore, fundamental to this book is the idea that the simple thrill of wine is one of the most enriching daily pleasures in which it is possible for humankind to indulge. My ambition here is to offer information which enhances, widens, deepens, and, since prohibitionary puritans still exist, legitimizes this enjoyment as a natural component of any thinking culture.

That said, who am I to deny someone the right to enjoy wine simply by hurling it into the nearest handy container and tossing it down the gullet? Such a tosspot will find these pages impossible to swallow, but the fact is that it is with this individual that we must begin our journey.

For, surely, all that is necessary to enjoy wine is simply to pour it into a glass and then down the throat? An alien sociologist with a sloppy observational technique will certainly report that this is so but the wine drinker, upon reflection, knows better. Of course you can quaff wine straight from the bottle, or with no more ceremony than raising a glass to your lips let it flood down the throat. No more strenuous athletic effort, no more profound sensory appreciation or intellectual consideration is necessary to achieve the entry of wine into the human digestive system.

By the same token of brutal insensitivity, though, you would also find nothing amiss in listening to recorded music at twice its proper speed. Have you ever heard 'Love Me Do' or the Goldberg Variations played at 75rpm when the recording is 33rpm? I recommend it. It is the auditory equivalent of throwing wine down the throat with no heed given to sight, smell, the feel and taste of the wine, or its soothing rhythm as it caresses the throat on the way down. Whether your taste is the Beatles or Bach, I suggest that no one is humanly capable of enduring for long the dispiriting, cacophonous distortion which speeded-up music (or slowed-down music for that matter) produces.

This is why this book came to be written. To love and fully appreciate wine, as it is properly to enjoy music, is to experience it at the right speed.

Could this book *really* open your eyes?

There are two ways to taste wine, just as there are two ways to negotiate Oxford Street in London's West End. If you only ever slurp wine, you will only ever achieve refreshment. If you merely slouch along Oxford Street, you will only ever see shops.

But certain wines can be appreciated in more considered fashion and deeper delights revealed, in the same way as strolling down Oxford Street and raising your sights will reveal some very interesting slabs of mercantile architecture at the higher levels. The vast majority of visitors and locals alike miss these adornments and are unaware of their existence. As a French novelist once remarked: to see things differently it is not necessary to encounter new landscapes but merely to see through new eyes. Wine drinkers, like any Oxford Street stroller, have all the faculties necessary for this newer, wider appreciation.

Wine tasting consists of the period from the contemplation of the wine in the glass, through its sensory appreciation, to its trickling (or gushing) down the throat. This can be a lengthy process — if the wine permits reflection and mature scrutiny. I do not pretend that every wine is like this: some — a rosé on a warm afternoon, say — merit no more than a simple flexing of the elbow, a cursory gargle and sniff, and ... hey presto! an empty glass.

This book is intended for anyone who is of sufficiently enquiring mind to want this tasting period to be effectively and unpretentiously enhanced. There is no other point to its publication.

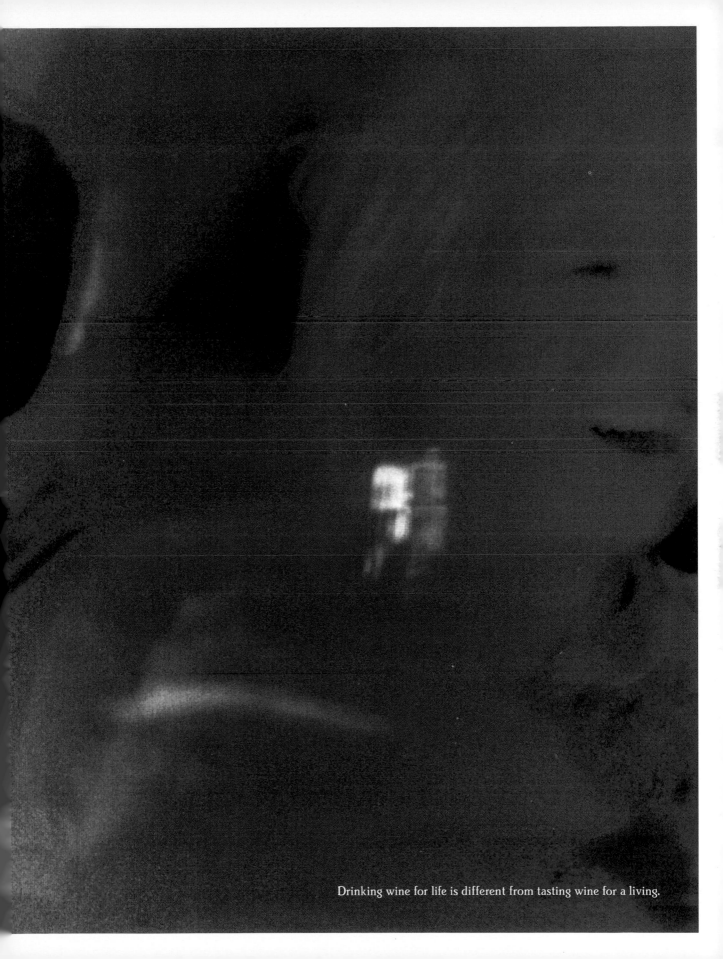

Drinking wine for life is different from tasting wine for a living.

In the end, I simply want my readers to feel encouraged, strengthened, less intimidated and, one day, confident enough to confront the charlatanism and fragrant hype which attend much of the world of wine and to recognize its hollowness. This may seem a contradictory claim to make for a book which invites its readers to stare longingly at wine, stick their noses in it, swill it round the mouth and make gargling noises as if fighting for breath, and, if so inclined spit it out or, if more relaxed, let it trickle down the throat and even enter the soul, but there it is.

The difference between tasting and enjoying

For me, the gulf which separates the concentrated procedures of the professional wine taster from the relaxed environment of the wine drinker is not huge. This admission disqualifies me, I suspect, from being considered a serious wine evaluator of the sort who, to please the snob, delves into microclimatical nuances and forensically dissects the soil type, the clone of the grape, the origin of the oak forest which supplied the wood for the barrel and the religion of the cooper who toasted the staves.

My primary concern when I first examine a wine professionally is this: will it give pleasure to the person who might buy it? How will it do this? How does it compare with similar wines offering similar expressions of fruit? And, lastly but most importantly, is it worth the money? These considerations give me licence to shoot off my mouth and tell the reader whether the wine is indeed able to answer the last question by giving it a rating from a single point to 20.

Now this means that I approach every wine in the hope that I will like it. I look for its virtues before I consider its faults (unless it immediately displays the latter in so evocatively revolting a way, either by means of a technical hiccup — too much sulphur, say — or tainted by its cork, that I am forced to ask for a fresh, untainted bottle to assess). This strikes me as an attitude which does not enjoy wide critical approbation. If there is a League of Critics, it surely presses upon its members the need to maintain a lofty disdain at all times. To go to the theatre, for example, out of enjoyment is not something the critic is necessarily asked to do; he is required to attend to scrutinize for lapses of taste and competence and may relish the opportunity to condemn.

This is the reason why so many tasters cannot abide cheap wine. They approach the bottle(s) with innate suspicion. The so-called 'great growths' or wines given a degree of international recognition are accorded a less prejudicial approach since the critic always hopes (some pray) that these wines will prove outstanding because this vindicates their reputations (and that of the tasters and critics who revere them).

In the final analysis I judge all wines by the criterion of value for money. Were expensive wines able convincingly and consistently to meet this simple criterion I would be happy to recommend more regularly to my readers that they purchase them. Too often such wines are inept and wickedly overpriced. There are fashions in wine which dictate price and distort genuine value, just as there are in food. For example, most Britons are familiar with the marketing history of the oyster. It was among the lowest forms of working-class food in the nineteenth century; the molluscs sold for pennies on stalls. Yet within a few years of my own father being born 100 years ago, in the closing year of the last century, the oyster was on its way to being elevated to a luxury dish for the so-called gourmet. Butter also enjoyed a similar incline in its social status (over a longer period). Whatever the crucial dietary value of these foods, the brutalities of fashion held greater sway than the realities of either health or sensory pleasure.

I hope this book may help to encourage the reader to be his or her own judge on real value and, by understanding more of the useful details of tasting and the enhanced pleasure this can provide, be more confident about whether spending £5, £10 or even £100 on a bottle of wine is justified.

Wine tasting — does it have a sixth sense?

There is, as I have discovered, a sense deliciously beyond the usual five (hearing, sight, smell, taste and touch) which only the shrewd wine drinker experiences.

You may question my assertion that every one of our senses is involved, to a greater or lesser extent, in enjoying a wine in the first place. However, I suggest that it is the sum total of the experience of our five senses, for those of us lucky enough to have all five intact, which provides the ultimate pleasure of the bottle. We hear the sound of the glass and the wine in the mouth (and to those stalwarts who insist on tradition there is romance in the plopping of the cork — of which abomination more later), we see the presentation of the bottle and the colour of the wine in the glass, we smell and taste the wine, and we not only feel its texture, we also enjoy the play of hand and glass. All this is cerebral and sensory.

But in addition there is the extraordinary sense of achievement, a cerebral refinement which adds an almost physical pleasure, to be experienced when we encounter a splendid wine. If that wine has not been expensively acquired, the pleasure is all the more intense.

This is a revolutionary, extremely modern idea to accept. The old-fogey connoisseur/wine taster accepts the importance of the senses of smell and taste, and to some degree sight, but little else. This hallowed trinity springs from snooty ways of buying, storing and appreciating wine. From it has developed much of the snobbery and status symbolism which still bedevils wine, making it not so much a simple pleasure as a hierarchical rite.

The modern wine drinker is not on first-name terms with a fusty wine merchant whose monocle is an apt image for his own unbalanced vision. The modern wine drinker does not have a cellar. The modern wine drinker does not wish to spend a fortune on wine. The modern wine drinker is master or mistress of pleasure, not slave to convention. The faculty loss implicit in the old notion of obeying the phoney rules of buying wine, which dictated that the drinker cede the responsibility for developing his or her own tastes to a slavish notion of social correctness, is disappearing.

This has led to the development of the sixth sense. Among other things, this enables the drinker to suss out terrific wines which don't cost a lot. Out of the compost heap of the accepted snotteries has grown the fresh, modern approach to appreciation and love of wine.

This approach brings a distinct, individual and peculiarly sensual pleasure to the drinking of wine. I won't hear a word said against it. It is being practised more regularly, even by a select few wine critics.

There are almost as many types of wine taster as there are wines. Which type are you?

It took me some years of tasting wines professionally before I realized that no one else tasted them in exactly the same way I did. I'm not talking about technique here, I am referring to focus or reasons for tasting. The question we must ask ourselves here is this: what am I looking for in this wine? It is how you answer this question which will determine the nature of your reaction to each and every wine you taste. Before you even behold a wine in its glass, let alone taste it, the framework of your response is already established by your predetermined attitude to wine.

When I taste my way through a retailer's range of, say, 100 wines my overall aim is to find as many wines as possible about which I can enthuse to my readers. I share their enthusiasm for delicious wines which don't cost a lot or which, if they do, are unspeakably marvellous and heart-stopping. My focus, then, is purity and richness of fruit balanced by price. Becoming a professional wine writer, after twenty-five years of dedicated wine study and wine drinking, did not involve me in any shift of focus. As a drinker I was always interested in bargains and in becoming a writer on the subject I did no more than give printed voice to my predilections.

When I taste wines these objectives, therefore, colour my responses. They sharpen my awareness of certain factors, they blunt my sympathies to others. This involves loss as well as gain. In never forgetting that I am writing for a readership which will take my ideas and recommendations seriously (though I hope a readership which also recognizes that I do not so take myself), I have lost the ability to differentiate between certain wine types and grape varieties, which a decade ago was a knack I took for granted.

What you are looking for determines what you see

My focus has changed. What is crucial for me today is to rate a wine accurately on a value-for-money basis, which means that when I taste it, it is being compared, on the same basis, with scores of others in my mind. Today we have wines from far more countries than ever before and therefore recognizing cabernet sauvignon when it has emanated from Zimbabwe, China, Brazil, Malta, let alone Argentina, Canada, Catalan, France or the Margaret River in Western Australia, is no longer the straightforward accomplishment it was in the good old days when cabernet sauvignon simply meant bordeaux (albeit divided into scores of sub-names and varietally blended). I no longer feel remotely excited about classifying wines according to their grapes and/or regional expression thereof; such judgements take second place a long way behind the value rating of the wine.

My taxonomic pigeon-holes contain fruit ranked according to criteria which do not have regional typicity or varietal expression as their defining characteristics. My nose and palate are connected to my own and my readers' pockets. When tasting a wine I compare it with as many others (worldwide) as can be instantly brought up on the screen of my consciousness by the software of my memory, and this leads me to rate the wine, through marks out of 20, as a value-for-money purchase — not, as would be the case with other wine commentators and critics, to consider it from the more romantic, in some cases even spiritual, perspective of provenance, nuance of varietal expression, and, in the case of wine writers whose subjectivity or intimacy with the wine maker or love of the region prevents a starkly clear view of the fruit in the bottle, past performance. I dare say I am sneered at by some who would say I am prosaic, utilitarian and boringly obsessed with the imponderable inexactitude of 'value for money' or what I have caused to be called superplonks. (I plead guilty to Auberon Waugh's charge that I am demotic. I want wine to be enjoyed by everyone, not kept as a lotion for cultural high priests.)

Tears at sundown.

It is important to recognize such predications as are implied by this confession, since we all taste wine for different reasons. One assumes that we all drink it for the same reasons: for the thrill it provides for the senses, for the pleasure it gives to those with whom we share it, and for its delightful alliance with the food that is perhaps on the plate in front of us. I never forget any one of these considerations. They are the bedrock of my approach. For how can it be that a wine which costs more than it should, or is a pathetic shadow of former greatness hiding behind a posh appellation, or which is a failure with food, can provide sufficient pleasure? It is only those to whom money means nothing, and whose palates reflect this indiscrimination, who can derive any pleasure or satisfaction from wines which are merely driven by the (often erotic) charge given them by astonishingly high price tags and vastly overpuffed reputations. One only has to look at what has happened to many great red and white burgundy names to recognize the truth of this. The region may be fighting back, and new wine makers are beginning to turn in some interesting fruit, but for years many burgundy drinkers who spent a lot were, perhaps deservedly if they couldn't tell the difference between the marvellous and mediocre, being ripped off.

To betray the evidence of one's own senses is to abandon common sense. But which two tasters share the same senses?

I am a bottle critic. I rate and describe specific vintages from individual vineyards or specific releases from wineries. Many other wine writers are not bottle critics. They report, often with vigour and insight, on the subject of wine, wine regions and wine makers. It is the difference between the renowned American wine critic Robert Parker and the English wine commentator Jancis Robinson. Like myself, Mr Parker comments on specific bottles and rates each one. He puts such considerations before all others (although, like me, he may well have a developed interest in particular wine regions, wine with food, certain grape varieties or wine makers, and would not be incapable of discoursing at length on these subjects if the whim struck or the opportunity in an appropriate context presented itself). Ms Robinson is more like a cultural critic and although she is possessed of a sound palate and developed tasting skills, her viewpoint, legitimized by her admiration for certain producers of wine and their vineyards and a love of wine in general, is one which considers other aspects of a wine than the brutal one of awarding it points out of 100 or out of 20. That is not her focus.

When we analyse wine we are speaking of wine; when we evaluate it we are speaking of ourselves

Professor Terry Eagleton, Oxford Professor of English Literature, inspired the above line of thought. It is a very pertinent consideration. It provides two sharp hooks, one for the analyst's hat and one for the enthusiast's.

My book is truly inviting the reader to develop a more analytic approach to wine but not one which then robs the subsequent drinking of it of its multi-faceted and relaxed pleasures. The one is not possible without the other, however. We must know why before we get to grips with the how.

Why are we tasting wine?

Wine experts taste for a variety of reasons. You are putting yourself in the position of developing and expressing expertise when you taste. So: ask yourself. What is my reason for tasting wine?

One: Is it to find a wine to take home to drink? Then your tasting focus will simply be to find a wine which suits your mood or the food you might later be eating.

Two: Is it to find wine to take home to cellar to drink at a later date? Then your tasting focus will be to scrutinize the impact of the wine on the palate, its acidity, its tannin, its sugar levels, to determine how it might age over time and develop in bottle. In these circumstances, you are likely to be a buyer of a case or several cases of the wine and the possessor of a proper cellar in which to allow the wine to mature in peace and quiet.

Three: Is it to ascertain the health of a wine ordered in a restaurant to go with the food? On the assumption that you know exactly what wine you want to go with the food you have ordered, you are tasting solely to determine that the wine is in a perfect state of drinkability (or, by being decanted, will reach its peak within an acceptable amount of time).

Four: Is it to discover if the wine is worth writing about? Then your focus may be widespread, indeed nebulous, and include factors as detached from the taste of the actual wine as the romance of the vineyard site or even the sense of humour of the wine maker.

Five: Is it to provide an accurate value-for-money rating? Then the focus here is as discussed above. It is not a tasting attitude which focuses on the wine detached from its price or removed from its competition.

Six: Is it to decide whether the wine should win a medal? Then you ignore all considerations except comparative performance in the glass, concentrating on the factors of smell, taste, structure and finish and how these compare with other candidates. You may well award marks for each aspect of the wine (colour, aroma, mid-palate, finish, structure, balance, varietal expression, and so on) and the sum of these marks will decide how the wine stacks up against other candidates.

Seven: Is it to determine if the wine has chemical faults? Focus here is ruthless. It considers such things as, among others, volatile acidity, balance, alcohol level, sugar, sulphur, cork taint, barrel contamination. These are specialized subjects and are dealt with in detail in the pages that follow.

Eight: Is it to see if the wine is a proper interpretation of its grape? Moving into an area like this calls for a concentrated focus, wide knowledge and a detailed memory.

Nine: Is it to ascertain if the wine is expressive or not of a particular region? A localized focus like this calls for a forgiving nature and extreme detailed knowledge. The most knowledgeable tasters here are the men and women who grow the grapes.

Ten: Are you tasting to decide on the component of a blend? This is one of the great unsung tasting skills, yet many times it rescues an undistinguished single varietal wine from obscurity. By blending wines from several grape varieties the wine maker can sometimes achieve not only a complete wine which is greater than its individual parts but also a more commercially saleable quantity of wine. This is a specialized tasting skill.

Eleven: Are you a *sommelier*, tasting (or more likely merely smelling) to determine the acceptability of a wine before offering it to the customer who has ordered it? In this case, you may be blind to certain faults in a wine because you feel so close to it. Many a *sommelier*, that is to say, the restaurant waiter in charge of wine, feels his wines are his children (especially if the restaurant has its own cellar and is not dependent upon a wholesale merchant for supplies of certain wines). Are we not all blind to the imperfections of our children? Sentiment clouds the wine expert's judgement just as sediment can the wine.

Twelve: Are you, as a retail wine buyer, tasting to find a wine you can sell for under £3.49? You are then tasting wines to find examples which fit into an already established range or meet a price point which will be broadly acceptable to customers. You may, in this situation, taste with a view to finding the least offensive bottles rather than outright stars.

I will stop here, at a round dozen. But this number does give an idea of how wide and complex is the arena of the wine-tasting focus. I daresay one could come up with scores of other reasons to taste.

The focus of each individual taster colours the perception of each wine and thus its very reality. Wine, like any other cultural artefact which impinges upon an appetite, is legitimately open to any interpretation compatible with reason.

A wine is a different experience to each individual taster. A wine is not a concrete absolutism; not a colour we can precisely and unerringly agree is red or orange or navy blue. Wine is a different phenomenon to each of its drinkers not only because each bottle may vary, however subtly, and each drinking occasion be hugely disparate, *but because each drinker has an individual focus which springs from the reason why that drinker tastes in the first place.* I am not referring here to mood, that variable which sometimes makes the wine we loved to death last week seem so jejune and unenthralling this. I refer to the actual viewpoint each taster brings to the experience of tasting each wine.

Who would deny each taster, mockery or disdain notwithstanding, the right to his or her private domain of self-focus? An individual bottle of wine has only a finite amount of time after it is opened before it stops being the wine its maker made or intended to make. In that time a dozen different tasters can visit it and arrive at a dozen different conclusions as to what it is or what it might be worth. The validity of each is only contradictable if what is palpably a contaminated bottle is claimed to contain nectar. Indeed, even on this basis there is room for disagreement since wine made from mouldy grapes can make sublimely honeyed and complex sweet whites. But who is to deny a taster with an aversion to rot his or her right to say that he or she finds such wine abnormal and revolting? (I am acquainted with such tasters.)

My own sensitivity to rot of the written rather than the vinified kind is no less strong. But what is rot and what is romance? Once we confess to being a wine lover we will commit to paper all manner of utter tosh in the febrile presumption that some chump will swallow it. We all come to wine in different circumstances and just as Tolstoy said, 'It is amazing how complete is the delusion that beauty is goodness,' it is no less amazing, and equally true, that each reaction to a wine is based on a personal affectation, delusion if you like, which each of us finds beautiful and based on goodness. It is a conspiracy of our own making. We conspire with our feelings and dupe our senses. Thus we do not find in a wine what someone else has found, and vice versa.

However, this is not to argue for consensus tasting. You can successfully blend wine; you cannot successfully blend opinions based on differing tasting foci. The only judgement on

The end of a day's tasting.

wine worth anything is that reached by the experienced motivated palate. *Your* palate. The committee, whether a pair of buffoons with pretensions to guide or an enclave of the half-educated conferring to scatter gongs, is death. That is why in the best of all possible worlds you should taste alone and judge alone — once, that is, you have evolved from the simple conviction that you know what you like to the more complex understanding of exactly *why* you like it. When that position is arrived at, your need for people like me or others at group tastings who may have helped your development is restricted to learning about wines you have not already tasted and how you might acquire the means to do so.

If you do not or cannot discover a focus for your tasting, you will, like certain woolly wine commentators and certain catch-all wine retailers, have no opinion worth listening to on individual wines. You will become, in effect, a committee spokesperson. Individual concentration as a professional taster is crucial. As Pamela Vandyke-Price, one of Britain's great veteran tasters and wine writers, wrote in her book *A Woman of Taste*: 'Tasting is an activity that demands one's entire attention. If you become irritated or angry during a tasting, the acidity will rise in your mouth and distort the taste of what otherwise may be well-balanced wines.'

So before you taste, ask yourself why it is you are tasting. Very soon, as you unite your focus with the delight of persevering at something so delightful as wine tasting, the question will become irrelevant. You will no more ask it of yourself than you would demand of Pete Sampras why he is wearing silly shorts and a floppy shirt and carrying what looks like a ski shoe in his hand.

You can enjoy wine without focusing on the reasons why you are doing so, but you cannot effectively taste wine without knowing why you are doing so. This is the root of the first class taster's technique.

The author crammed into the space normally reserved for his bike.

Bark that can be worse than a bite.

Two

Who needs corkscrews? (Or in some cases, who needs corks screwing up wines?)

2 The Second Lesson

(Don't taste the wine, taste the cork)

Before we pull the cork, however, there is an important check we should make. A vital clue to the condition of the wine within the bottle is provided by the gap between the level of the wine in the bottle and the bottom of the cork. There is a technical term for this gap: the ullage.

One: The ullage. In any modern wine bottle the ullage should never be so great that the wine laps the shoulders of the bottle. No more than an inch should gape between the top of the wine and the bottom of the cork when the bottle is held upright. If the gap is wider, excessive evaporation of the wine may have taken place (in an old wine) and rendered the contents of the bottle unfit to drink. With some bottles, the capsule (the foil over the bottle top) is so long it obscures the level of the wine. This is fine, though since sometimes even the most sophisticated modern bottling machinery fills the odd bottle too full and the wine is, unbeknownst to the purchaser, in full contact with the bottom of the cork; this may cause embarrassment when the cork is extracted. There's nothing wrong with the contact itself — a cork should be a totally neutral seal after all — but care should be exercised because as you pull the cork an amount of wine will inevitably shoot up as the cork slides through the neck. In the Knees-Bent-I'm-A-Real-Man position, designed to emphasize the phallic symbolism of corkscrew insertion and cork expulsion, wine from an overfilled bottle will undoubtedly shower over the expeller's trousers. No more than such an athlete deserves, you may say. However, if the capsule is fully removed it is easy to see how high the wine level is and such an accident can be avoided. For some drinkers, the spilling of the odd spot of wine may be part of the ritual.

There is a device (patent pending I believe) which measures ullage. It is called the Mirrington Level Indicator (available to buy from Rare and Fine Wines Limited of London, TEL: 0181 960 1995) and is designed for use by wine investors and auctioneers. It is made of thick Perspex with convexly shaped sides which variously fit the neck and shoulder of any bordeaux- or burgundy-shaped bottle or magnum. You place the side of the sheet against the bottle and read off whether the wine corresponds to one of eight levels from HF (high fill) to BLS (below shoulder). Frankly, I regard the device as a tiresome irrelevance since any knowledgeable buyer or seller can take one look at a wine bottle and decide, bearing in mind its age, whether the wine is badly ullaged, or acceptably ullaged as one would expect for a wine of its age.

Two: The cork. More important to the condition of the wine is the condition of the cork. And the latter's condition, alas, is only discernible (apart from visible deterioration via crumbling in a very ancient bottle) when a corkscrew has removed it. And thus we enter the hideous realms of uncertainty.

There is one thing which comes between a drinker and a perfect glass of wine, and that is that blessed bung made of cork. The cork may be the second lesson in wine tasting but it is of primary importance. The cork can be saint; it can be sinner. To decide which, you have to taste it, that is to say, smell the cork to get a deep sensory impression of it, before you do anything else. A cork is an astonishingly antiquated object to find in the neck of a bottle of modern wine. It is, none the less, an object endowed with mystical powers. This is because it adds the element of chance to the bottle. If it were a perfect answer to the problem of preventing air from entering a wine bottle, if it was not made from an often contaminated material which taints the liquid, if it could be removed without ceremony and without the need to use a special instrument (itself a ceremonial device), all the romance of wine would simply relate to the wine itself. But cork, because of snobbery, usage and historical precedent, not only claims some of this romance for itself but often dominates proceedings on the many occasions when it forms a feeble seal and acts as a fruit thief.

You should smell the bottom of the cork immediately upon removing it from the bottle. You should either smell wine or nothing at all. Any 'alien' or 'off' smells, any hint of rancidity, mushroominess or cardboardiness should alert you to the possibility that the wine is not in a perfect state to drink. In cases of extreme pollution, the taint upon the cork is sufficiently recognizable to permit the individual holding the bottle – if he or she is a restaurant waiter or *sommelier* – immediately to withdraw the wine and fetch a fresh bottle. Serving perfect wine is the prime job of *sommeliers*, yet it is an area of contention which continues to bedevil the pleasures of every wine drinker who regularly buys wine and/or eats out.

Three: Plastic cork or screwcaps? The answer to cork taint is simple and, led by Marks and Spencer with their plastic corks and Tesco with its introduction of screw-capped wines, the UK's most prominent wine supermarkets and retailers are at last addressing the problem seriously. Wine producers, too, are looking at ways of replacing cork with guaranteed taint-free corks made from plastic polymers, although in concert with many wine makers I would prefer to see all wines sealed with screwcaps. Screw-caps are a more fool-proof, taint-free way of sealing wine, no oxidization takes place through the seal and therefore (barring a mechanical fixing error) the wine ages without outside help. Wine is kept fresher and stays in a drinkable condition for longer with a screw-cap. The wine matures but is dependent solely on the bulk of alcohol and the chemicals in the bottle to do this. No wonder so many wine makers like the idea. It is not, alas, a pretty sight as far as some people are concerned. For them the screw-cap suggests a second-rate product into which little thought has been put; paradoxically where wine is concerned the very opposite is true. For me, the sight of a screw-cap immediately promotes the idea of a fault-free wine.

The romance of wine is surely in the liquid, not in its method of closure. It is sheer laziness, indifference, sloppiness and ritualized claptrap that have kept the cork in wine bottles. It is the laziness of a cork industry which is clod-hopping and undynamic. It is the indifference of wine merchants who erect barriers to customers' expression of dissatisfaction. It is the sloppiness of wine producers who have sealed their wines with cork for years in the full knowledge that a proportion of their customers will inevitably receive sub-standard wine. And under it all, crawling beneath the whole rotten edifice, is the supportive attitude of the wine snob who positively loves the degree of chance which natural cork confers on wine because it makes wine knowledge more difficult to acquire and provides thornier barriers for the novice to negotiate. It is only because men have been the main buyers and openers of wine for so long that the cork has lasted this far – to the end of the twentieth century. If women had their way, screw-caps would have been in full use since about the time war-time rationing ended in Britain.

Four: The big debate. The incidence of wine tainted by corks has become one of the hottest subjects under discussion in the wine world. The discussion has gathered momentum because of the increasing popularity of young, fresh New World wines which are fruit-dominated and, being made to be drunk young, show up any bruising of this friskiness and fruitiness. With older, more tannic reds designed to age for decades and sweet or sweet/acid whites which will also last for very many years, I am of the unshakeable conviction that it is the cork in these wines which is the cause of so much differentiation between the same wines of the same vintage from the same vineyard. If you read the tasting notes of any taster who regularly gets to grip with old wines — twenty, thirty, fifty, eighty years old — there is very rarely a consistency of observation in this respect; each wine, though supposedly part of the same close-knit family, will receive a different descriptive accolade (or denigration) and, although admittedly these notes are made many months or even years apart, a feeling is nevertheless conveyed that different wines are being written up. The romantic will say, 'Well, this is part of the charm and romance of wine', but I consider this a fraudulent conclusion. Romance comes from the object of desire: the wine; it cannot come from the packaging. Otherwise, are we not simply duping ourselves? Why should a wine seal be a gamble with excellence? Why should one wine of the same batch be great and the next mediocre or not-so-great? This is not romance. It is delusion. With a guaranteed taint-free method of wine closure, plastic corks or screw-caps, the wine would be permitted to age unbruised by the bullying natural tree-bark cork. This would apply as much to wine made to age for years, as to wine created to be consumed within a couple of years of its harvest.

Five: How to spot a corked wine. The only sure way for the inexperienced taster to check whether a wine is faulty is to compare two bottles, one with a smelly cork, the other with a non-smelly cork. This is hardly practical if you are in a restaurant and not sure of your opinion or if you have opened a single bottle at home or been asked to open a bottle at a friend's. I now never drink or comment upon a wine which is faulty when I am served it at a dinner party at a friend's home. It is too embarrassing for the host. I keep my mouth shut so I don't have to drink the wine or pass an opinion (unless pressed).

The reverse is true when I am in a restaurant. In thirty-three years of eating out, the number of occasions when the serving by a waiter of a faulty wine has led to an instant and equable replacement when the fault has been pointed is about equal to those times when the waiter, after my polite refusal to accept it, has smelt or tasted the wine (rarely the cork unless I have insisted on it) and found little to complain about. A good *sommelier* always asks the customer to smell the cork (if that *sommelier* has done so already, and smelt the wine, and considered both in a fit state). Be confident in this situation. Many *sommeliers* are simply wine salesmen or so in love with their cellars that they cannot see faults. If the cork is not perfect, if it has tainted the wine, the pressure to buy is immediately lifted from the customer's shoulders. Do not accept less than perfect wine. I believe that diners-out are regularly served tainted wine in full knowledge of the wine waiter who, reckoning he can get away with it, simply lets the bottle pass.

A corked wine can smell, subtly but spoilingly, of any one of several identifiable aromas:

One: Cardboard. (That flat, gently musty tang.)
Two: Vegetation. (Not fresh, but rotted, cabbagey — an echo of compost.)
Three: Mushrooms. (An unnatural earthiness which is not a tannic phenomenon.)
Four: Staleness. (Reminiscent of central-heating radiators.)
Five: Foxiness. (Dustiness, like old unaired cupboards.)
Six: Insipidity. (A red with an edge of unattractive sourness, but this is a taste sensation not an olfactory one and so one of the above would be noticeable first.)

These six criminals are members of a much larger gang of 'off' wine smells which live within a tainted cork, and a full membership list of smell impressions, as arrived at scientifically, might encompass scores more. The overall impression of a 'corked' wine is, however, roughly the same on the nose: the wine isn't fresh, it isn't as fruity as it should be (it is marred), it is tainted.

Will you pull out a plum?

Whatever the characteristic of this taint, it is an indication of a wine which has been affected by the cork taint known as 2-4-6 trichloranisole and which the cork industry seems unable to eradicate. This taint is different from other 'off' odours such as:

One: Oxidation. (A sharpness due to air intrusion.)
Two: Volatility. (The development of acetic acid bacteria which give the wine a vinegary edge.)
Three: Excessive sulphur. (A slight burning sensation or a burnt match aroma.)
Four: Egginess. (The presence of hydrogen sulphide evoking the smell of bad eggs.)
Five: Onions. (An ethyl mercaptan which also derives from hydrogen sulphide.)
Six: Gassiness. (The presence of carbon dioxide, not always attractive in a wine intended to be still, which manifests itself as a prickle on nose and tongue.)

These and other factors affecting the way a miserable specimen of wine may smell and taste are discussed in Chapter 13 of this book.

Certain American restaurant customers, if they come across the book *The Man Who Ate Everything* by the magazine food critic Jeffrey Steingarten, will be told that there is nothing to be learned from scrutinizing a wine cork. Having enrolled in the New York Professional Service School, which trains waiters and *sommeliers*, Mr Steingarten obtained a diploma, thus proving his credentials, and he writes as a result of this schooling: 'When you order wine and the waiter puts the cork down in front of you ignore it — you cannot learn anything by smelling or squeezing the cork.' If *sommeliers* trained at the NYPSS have been similarly instructed to ignore the cork, heaven help anyone who sends back a restaurant wine in the Big Apple!

Send the culprit packing!

It is impossible, in a book, to teach anyone to detect unfailingly the presence of TCA, as trichloranisole is known. It can only be picked up through experience. Yet having said that, it is not always true that experienced professional wine buyers are consistent spotters of the problem. TCA is like a thief in the night who steals only a few biscuits from the cookie jar. He does not plunder the lot so that suspicions are instantly aroused. He steals stealthily and slyly. Can you be sure any cookies at all have been stolen? Not unless you are fully aware of exactly how many the jar contained the moment before you went to bed.

I have been served faulty wine countless times at wine merchants' tastings, wine checked for quality before I entered the room. I have even been offered wine fouled up with TCA, admittedly very subtly, by the wine-maker himself (never, I must say, herself). I have even heard of expert British drinkers finding the *gendarmes* being called when refusing to pay for faulty, and undrunk, wine in a French restaurant where the *sommelier* insisted on adding the cost of the bad bottle to the final bill. I myself was harassed well beyond good manners and common sense by both waiter and *sommelier* (not to be confused, by the way, with the term *sommeiller* which pertains to doziness), then by the chef-proprietor himself when he finally emerged scowling from his kitchen, when I refused to accept a bottle of tainted wine at one of Oxford's more prominent restaurants. At one posh eaterie in Soho where I was compelled to refuse to accept two successively faulty bottles, the *sommelier* panicked and went apoplectic with displeasure. The French, in my experience, have a particular problem with TCA. They do not seem to realize it exists. All French wine, certain Frenchmen believe, is perfect, cork taint often being confused in their minds with woodiness or tannicity.

Is it any wonder I campaign for plastic corks and screw-caps?

A corked wine is rarely manifestly vile. It simply isn't the real thing. Its complexities are muffled; its brilliant edge blunted. It's like listening to sport on radio. A corked wine is often so subtly altered that it resembles the genuine article sufficiently convincingly to make us believe that is the way it truly is. One is reminded of James Joyce's comment about the translation of a text being 'the other side of the tapestry'. A subtly corked wine is a bad translation; unable to show us the true face of the artefact it offers only an approximation. It is a pity wine waiters are not more aware of it or even sympathetic to the problem.

A friend of mine was eating at a famous fish restaurant and ordered a bottle of chardonnay. It did not seem right; not so much woody as positively arboreally tangy.
This wine is surely corked, my friend said to herself. She raised the matter with the waiter.

Friend: I wonder if this wine is corked. It doesn't seem right.
Waiter: Have you cleaned your teeth in the past twenty-four hours?
Friend: Well, what do you think?!
Waiter: Actually we don't recommend this wine with fish. It's very strongly flavoured.

Apart from the waiter's attitude beggaring belief and his enquiry into my friend's dental hygiene being either an attempt at a bad joke or, more likely, sheer cheeky stupidity, one is also entitled to ask what a fish restaurant is doing with wines on its list which the waiter, who is a representative of the management, considers too strong for fish. The name of this wine has been forgotten, alas, but I believe it was Australian. There is no Australian chardonnay too strong for all fish — although a delicate poached sole would be overpowered by certain barrel-fermented Aussie monstrosities — and so the miscreant waiter was wrong on this count too.

The most spectacular sending back of a wine I know of concerns one of the larger British supermarkets which received a truckload of beaujolais and, their buyer, as always, routinely tasted sample bottles. So many were tainted by their corks that the supermarket sent back the whole truckload — 18,000 bottles. I am led to believe that wine maker is now taking legal action against his cork supplier.

You and I do not, of course, have the clout of a supermarket that deals in tens of millions of bottles of wine a year. Nevertheless, it is the single bottle in front of us at lunch or dinner that is important. It can take the edge off an enjoyable meal if it is not replaced, or an instant refund offered, without demur. Developing the ability to spot a faulty wine and building the confidence to ensure it is not you who pays for it is an important wine-tasting skill.

Discuss the problem. You're the one paying the bill

I cannot see much difference, in terms of solving the problem, between sending back a dish you might consider uneatable (too salty, too rare, cold when it should be hot) and a wine which is faulty. Why should anyone fear making a fool of himself or getting his head bitten off? It is only the ignorance and prejudice of the purveyors of wine that stand in the way of simple justice being done. It is one more dreadful indictment of the snobbery attached to wine and the barriers wilfully erected to its enjoyment that it should even enter the head of the customer that he or she might be embarrassed when querying a wine's condition or refusing to accept it.

The biggest stumbling block to the identifying of a faulty, TCA-contaminated cork is that in the vast majority of cases the wine is not so powerfully disgusting to smell that it would be apparent even to an olfactory imbecile that there is something wrong with it. On the basis of my postbag over the past decade and my personal experience with encountering corked wines, most bottles which are duff merely have an edge missing. The TCA in the cork has not rendered the wine impossible to drink; merely impossible to regard as fruity as it should be. Thus, either the drinker considers himself or herself unworthy of the wine (rather than the other way around) or he or she simply shrugs and says, 'Not as terrific a wine as I was led to believe — what a pity.'

Both these reactions concern me. The first is endemic to wine appreciation in that the subject is regarded as so mysterious and arcane that many people think either that a wine which is subtly faulty is not to their liking or that they are unable to appreciate its greatness because they lack the skill to understand it. I do not claim that every great wine or even wine I would regard as terrific or rate highly must therefore immediately be considered great by everyone else. We cannot ride roughshod over the area of personal preference here; without question certain experienced drinkers dislike the gaminess of real pinot noir, find uncongenial the paraffin undertones of certain mature rieslings, and reckon unpalatable the fleshy vigour of a highly wrought Australian chardonnay. And so on. But when drinkers choose a wine they do not pick on a wine style to which they are indifferent; so when they do, say, like Rhône reds and order accordingly and, shall we say, expensively, then they have a right to find a pleasurable bottle, notwithstanding the vicissitudes of vintages, rather than a specimen which is less than as thrilling as it ought to be because it has been contaminated, very subtly, by TCA.

So it is that many a reader of mine must have shaken his head over a wine I have raved about and which he has purchased in expectation of thrills galore, only to be confronted by fair to middling fruit of no obvious excitement. Does the wine smell awful? Not a bit of it. It's merely a tad dull. Poor old Gluckie or Superwanker or whatever I get called has lost his marbles over this one; had his tongue too firmly stuck in his cheek.

I do not resent the implication that at times I may lack judgement. I protest when wines which I recommend are going to fail to live up to my description. I want my readers to drink the same wine as me. The same wine I have written about. The same wine, with the same fruit, with the same capacity to thrill. The incidence of contaminated cork prevents this.

And another thing: corks can be as individualistic as humans — no two are the same

Even if the wine is not contaminated there is often variation in the quality of each and every cork in a single batch which goes into, say, a bottling line run of 10,000 bottles. To imagine that each and every cork cut from the same section of bark from the same oak tree is exactly the same is as erroneous as believing that every child from the same parents is identical.

The price difference in corks, which vary in quality (and cost from 3p to 30p each), is also enormous. The most expensive is not always the most neutral and least harmful to the structure of the fruit in the wine. I took part in a tasting experiment in 1998 in which ten corks of varying prices were each placed in a small, sterilized plastic flask which was then filled with fresh white wine, a pinot gris, directly from the tank. The amount of wine in contact with the cork was some seventy-six times what it would be with a normal bottle, but since the flasks were to be opened and the contents tasted after only five days this exaggerated contact was essential in order for smell and taste nuances to be recognizable by a human nose and palate. The dramatic results revealed the influences at work on a wine by what is supposed to be a totally clean seal.

Amazing what you can see in a wine once you learn how to smell it.

Of the ten pinot gris, each acquired a different colour, from very pale gold to yellow; the flavours ranged from outright TCA, through stale butterscotch to caramel; several examples showed an unattractive pungency of alcohol; one smelt of ripe cheese; another of sun tan cream. All from a supposedly neutral method of stoppering wine! A representative of the winery which supplied the wine, somewhat shocked by the findings, said that 'A couple of these wines would, if they had been conventionally bottled, be almost undrinkable after six months in contact with their corks.'

Let's get rid of tree bark in wines

The sooner wines are sealed with plastic, or screw-capped, the better. Nothing but outworn tradition is standing in our way.

Wine tasting can hardly be described as a science. Neither can it be characterized as an art — not if a small proportion of the pictures on view are hung upside down without anyone noticing or complaining about it. I don't think this is outside the scope of this book. It affects the taste of wine.

So complain about it if the wine you have purchased doesn't taste as you think it should. Corked wine would disappear overnight if everyone who had been cheated of pleasure in this way made a fuss. The pressure on retailers and restaurants would be so huge that they would have to act to ensure taint-free wine.

One forlorn hope of mine is that a sympathetic food scientist will discover that TCA in certain doses is poisonous to humans. Cork would then be banned from being in contact with food (and wine is classifiable as food). Is there any qualified individual reading this who feels inclined to conduct the research? Failing this, we drinkers will just have to wait until screw-caps and plastic corks become the norm. Both can be recycled. What are we waiting for?

The last word. Let the cork speak

As a matter of record, Amorim, the Portuguese company which is the world's biggest supplier of corks, strongly defends the quality of its own product, while admitting that many other smaller cork suppliers may not be so conscientious. The company believes that TCA originates much of the time in winery water and not in the cork. However, if this were true, complete batches of wine would be corked, not just random bottles. I have discussed Amorim's notion with dozens of wine makers and they have, with one exception, scornfully rejected it. The exception was an oenologist at the Institut Oenologique de Champagne, Pierre-Yves Bournerias, who pointed out to me that there is a similarity between chlorine, the cleaning agent of raw tree bark before it becomes cork, and the agent used to remove the tannin from fermentation and storage tanks. ' There can be problems with cleaning agents. Chlorine is the one which molecularly has the structure to cut the tannins from inside the steel tanks and if it is not thoroughly rinsed off afterwards it can very very lightly coat the steel. Your cork supplier could be right about TCA in winery water — if the winery isn't careful.' Monsieur Bournerias also pointed out that TCA has been found in the wooden beams of cellar ceilings and within the pallets used to store wine.

However, in my experience thus far, and also in the anecdotal experience of every wine taster, wine grower and wine maker with whom I have discussed it, no one has yet encountered a TCA-faulty wine which has been screw-capped or plastic-corked. Cork, then, still remains the prime suspect in the mystery entitled *Who Killed the Fruit in the Bottle?* For my money, cork is as guilty as hell.

But . . . has Jose Neiva come to cork's rescue?

Late in 1998, I received a most illuminating letter from Lindsay Talas, product development manager in Tesco's wine-buying department. It read as follows: 'Another exciting development in Portugal is Jose Neiva's work on an innovative solution to TCA cork taint. Traditionally two kinds of cork treatment were used: first calcium chloride and oxalate were used, but this worsened the taint; later hydrogen peroxide was used in liquid form, but this interfered with the cork tissue and led to wine leaking out of the bottles. Jose developed a treatment using ozone gas which has the advantage that it penetrates the cork tissue more easily without changing the structure, and it acts as a non-toxic disinfectant and a deodorant. He tested the treatment under laboratory conditions and trialled this treatment for six years in one of his wineries. During this period there were no incidences of cork taint of the wines bottles with the treated corks. Jose has now patented this treatment and recently sold it to the Amorim group . . . We are extremely committed to supporting solutions that will rid the industry of TCA taint. We are currently investigating this method and hope to further increase the number of wines within our range that we can guarantee will not be affected by cork taint.'

The exciting word here is the word guarantee. Early days, true, and only a small number of wines, for the foreseeable future, would be subject to it. But is this the beginning of the end of cork taint? My fingers are crossed.

The Neiva initiative is not the only one involving the cork industry's sudden drive to eliminate taint. A cork called Altec, produced by the world's second largest cork producer, Sabate (which has its head office near Perpignan), is finding its way on to the UK market in certain bottles and although no guarantee of 100 per cent purity is given the results so far seem to justify the company's confidence in the product. The Altec cork is based on the ridding of the natural cork base of all lignin content, that is to say the woody constituents which harbour the taint. In the company's own words: 'Altec corks have been developed by uniquely removing a major part of the lignin/wood content from ordinary cork and replacing most of it with more pure cork.' Not a cheap process, and it isn't perfect, but it is a step in the right direction.

The right tool . . .

Three

. . . in the right hand.

3 The Transparent Go-Between

(The virtues and vices, pains and pleasures of the wine glass)

I do not see any need to dwell here on the history of the wine glass, short though it is (our European ancestors drank from everything, from a bull's horn to an earthenware jug). Certainly in the beginning wine was glugged without ceremony, ancient Roman orgiastic niceties notwithstanding. By the time wine had acquired a wider franchise and the fruits of the burgeoning industrial revolution were falling more thickly to the ground, the old glassblowers of Venice from whose lips came the finely engraved drinking vessels of royalty and aristocracy had mundane rivals in the shape of the more prosaically blown tumblers and goblets of the inn and late eighteenth-century merchant-class dinner table.

As the idea became established that a best set of crystal, amongst the prosperous, was essential equipage, there developed a definite move towards preferring different styles of glass for different wines. Today, there is a plethora of glass shapes. But in essence one thing has never changed over the past few hundred years: glass, being transparent, is preferable to other materials. One thing that has changed, however, is the decided preference of the experienced wine drinker for clear, stemmed glasses above all others. Engraved or coloured glasses offer translations of the wine's colour and are despised as parvenu and flashy.

Yet with all these civilized advances there is still the one unsuitable glass out of which everyone has drunk at some stage in his wine-loving career.

This is the transparent object called the Paris Goblet by those in the catering profession. It pretends to be a wine glass. It is squat enough and thick enough to withstand the rigours of a dishwasher without its stem snapping and it is to be found in thousands of establishments throughout the length and breadth of every country which has restaurants.

The Paris Goblet. Please kiss it goodbye.

Under no circumstances can The Paris Goblet be used to enjoy wine. It is the universal pub wine glass. You may drink from it, true. But equally you can also drink from an Oxford brogue. Why is this glass so uncongenial? Because it cramps the wine's performance — in much the same way as the Oxford would if worn on the foot of a squash player. The Paris Goblet is like a cello two strings of which cannot be tuned. You may find such a glass useful for optical grit removal but not for the proper appreciation of wine.

Start as you mean to go on

There are two things to say about any wine glass. First, choose the right one for the wine. Second, always start by smelling the glass before any wine enters it.

Dealing with the second, and very important, point first, let me offer an anecdotal example to explain why a brief olfactory examination is essential.

I was in a Pizza Express a few months before this book was published and I asked for a glass of a wine which, upon smelling it, I could see was clearly contaminated. For a moment I thought, 'bad cork'. Then I smelt my children's cola glasses. They were also contaminated. Washing-up liquid was the culprit, and after the problem had been pointed out to the waiter, and he had smelt other clean glasses, the washer-up was summoned to return all the glasses in the restaurant to the kitchen for a thorough rinsing.

The lesson of this prosaic anecdote is clear. Never pour wine into a glass without smelling it first. Even at professional wine tastings I have discovered soapy glasses or ones which have so recently been removed from their cardboard boxes that they are faintly musty.

Such glasses not only dramatically affect the wine for the worse, they also inhibit the formation of the effervescence in a sparkling wine. Glasses in your own home should always be thoroughly rinsed in clean warm water and not stored with their stems in the air and the rims in contact with a shelf surface. Always dry glasses with a dry tea-towel.

Glasses can also smell slightly musty if not stored correctly. The bowls of glasses should be exposed to the air and not kept where they can pick up odours from anything else, however seemingly benign. Ideally, glasses should be suspended from racks by their stems but few people, including me, go to this trouble. I do, however, always ensure that glasses are not stored with their stems uppermost and the bowls on a shelf or work surface. (I once had to choose my words carefully to explain to a hostess I barely knew why I could not pour into her exquisite glasses the wonderful wine in front of us because they had picked up, deliciously but fatally, the faint hint of coriander from being kept in her spice cupboard.) Okay. The glasses are clean and smell of nothing. So which one should we choose?

For the regular professional tasting of wine, there is an accepted tasting glass meeting International Standards Organization specifications and tolerances, and it is called the ISO glass. It is widely used in France and I've also come across it at professional wine shows in Australia and in tasting rooms in Spain, Italy and Germany. It is something like a large sherry glass.

The elusive glass

It is not easy to find out from whom ISO glasses can be purchased. My first attempts to discover a manufacturer let alone any suppliers met with little success. The first professional wine buyer I asked about the glass, Elizabeth Robertson of Safeway, told me, 'We use a similar glass for professional tastings but not the approved ISO one. In any case, when we first got hold of a box of some ISO glasses, years ago now, we were astonished to find a set which varied in dimensions and thickness of glass. We thought it a bit of a joke that it was called a "standard" tasting glass in the circumstances.'

Unlikely, then, that it was John Jenkins & Co which supplied this box. This company, a wholesaler I finally tracked down, supplies first-class ISO glasses, which meet the standard specifications, to wine shops and merchants and also to Debenhams where you can spend as little as £2.95 or as much as £5.50 on one (there are three glasses of differing quality in the range). The prices may have changed since this book's publication of course, but the company is very helpful and can be contacted on 01730 821811.

The ISO glass was designed in France several decades ago and, like any tool perfected by use over the years, is excellent for the job it does. That is to say, for the professionally engaged taster, who may well be going through anything from a dozen to a dozen dozen wines during a working day, this light, easy-to-handle glass permits sufficient wine (less than one third of the 200+ millilitres the glass can hold), to be contained, for examination purposes, yet none

A glass for young reds

A glass for fresh young whites
(especially young rieslings)

A glass which suits young
chilled reds and chardonnays
(and the richer white grapes)

Glasses fit for the wine.

A glass to suit all
sorts of whites

A general red or white
quaffing glass

A glass for more mature reds

will spill when agitated. The height of the bowl allows the nose to be inserted without breathing wine up the nostrils (not a pleasant experience the one time I did, cacknosedly, let it happen). The aroma is funnelled nosewards by the glass's shape and the stem is the perfect height to permit the fingers to grasp and spin the wine.

A working glass is not a leisure glass

When I drink wine at home outside my tasting room (a cupboard-sized kitchen attached to my study), I seem to use no more than half-a-dozen different glasses. If they have anything in common it is that each permits wine to be swirled without spilling and the contents can easily be smelt from a bowl which is shaped for optimum appreciation of colour and bouquet. Each glass is also free of any ornamentation and completely clear. I abominate decoration on a wine glass, except when slurping Moselle in certain bars in the region, and coloured ones should only be filled with fresh flowers. I also must admit that I like two kinds of very large red wine glass, each of which can take a third of a bottle yet still permit me to agitate the contents and enjoy the aroma without showering myself. When I am wrapped up in a book or watching TV or listening to music I am thus not required constantly to replenish my glass.

For serving wine at dinner, whether this is by myself, or with the family, or with a bunch of friends at what passes for a dinner party in our house, I employ glasses for specific types of wine. I find a small number of broad styles sufficient. But there are scores of different sorts of wine and indeed spirit glasses. The Austrian super-perfectionist George Riedel, for instance, has a glass company which makes some seventy different ones, among them individual glasses for certain grape varieties, including gewürztraminer, young cabernet sauvignon(!) and chardonnay. There is even a choice of Riedel glass for cognac XO and cognac VSOP. (Imagine the shame of it being bruited abroad that you were serving VSOP in the XO glass! You'd have to wear sackcloth and retire to a hermitage.) Herr Riedel has even designed a glass for Beaujolais Nouveau — which just shows how lampoonably risible the subject can become since, in my experience, this bloated, much-hyped confection hasn't been worth putting in any sort of glass for two decades.

Personally, I like Riedel's champagne glass (404/8 is the product reference number), the 416/1 riesling glass, the 400/16 red burgundy glass, the 404/5 white wine glass, and his all-purpose so-called 'Gourmet' glass which is based on a design for chianti. Anyone who buys both Riedel's champagne glass and vintage champagne glass, and uses them faithfully for their designated uses, has both a palate stratospherically higher than mine (not to mention a matching bank balance) and a generous tolerance of sheer unadulterated pretension.

The company has also launched what it calls 'the ultimate tasting glass' with a fat hollow stem. I find it absurd, clumsy, and irrelevant. It is best used to display a single rose than to contain any drinkable liquid.

Without doubt, wine tastes better in a glass designed to enhance its nuances rather than mask them. Hence my dismissal of the Paris Goblet. But there comes a point where the difference between various glasses is like that between a Bosendorfer and Steinway, whether the pianist is Gould or Shelley, whether the venue is the Queen Elizabeth Hall or the Carnegie Hall, and whether the composer is Mozart or Bach. I daresay there is a music lover somewhere who has a preference for one of these two pianos and an opinion about the performer — but wine is not so giddy with complexities (whatever snobs might do to try to make it so).

The glasses in which I serve wine at home come from the Vino Grande range made by the German Spiegelau company, sold by Nachtmann UK, and I am very happy to acknowledge that the company supplied the glasses for this book and also pays me for sponsoring this range in UK shops (though I used these inexpensive glasses before I was aware that one day I might get them for free). I regularly use certain of this range of glasses, shown on pages 50 to 51. For serving wine, these practical yet elegant vehicles are enough for me (and for my dishwasher, although I handwash the fatter glasses because I fear breakage).

I firmly resist the notion that we must try too hard where glasses are concerned. It is enough to recognize that just as you don't turn up on a golf course with a croquet mallet you don't serve a rich red wine in a glass meant for sparkling wine. But does young cabernet sauvignon really deserve its own glass? That is codswallop. The wine would taste just as good out of any simple, generous-bowled, red wine glass. (Shorn of its pretentious detail it is amazing, in fact, how much more relaxed and thereby enjoyable wine drinking becomes. Who wants to fret over the 'right' glass?)

Four eyes, one wine.

Four

4 The All-Seeing Eye

(What can you read in a glass of wine?)

We are about to taste. What are we looking for? We are tasting the wine to establish certain aspects of its make-up. Aspects each of which contributes to the degree of delight, or indifference or disgust, that wine will convey. Only then do we evaluate it: in my case as a working wine writer; in your case, perhaps, simply as a wine lover who wishes to enhance his or her love of it.

We taste, we examine, we scrutinize the wine in a glass to determine five broad criteria:

One: Its colour. Is this thrilling? Is it compellingly golden or a gorgeous purple? Or is it uninspiringly yellow or a lack-lustre red? Is it merely unremarkable? At this primary tasting stage, we are already putting all our senses on alert via the single initial sense of sight.

Two: Its smell. Does the wine's aroma (or bouquet) suggest a healthy wine? Is it fault-free? Does it immediately suggest a grape variety? Certain analogous fruits? Is it an inviting, delicious, worthy-of-further-investigation aroma or is it simply okay? As this olfactory knack develops you will, as revealed in later pages, discover a symphony of notes, melodious or discordant, and an abundance of clues as to the wine's provenance and worth from which you may derive pleasure or pain or dismiss with a mere shrug of the shoulders.

Three: Its taste. As the wine encounters the taste receptors in the mouth, what is the immediate sensation? Is it richness? Is it tartness? Is it a dry wine? Is it sweet? Is it off-dry? Is the wine suggestive of a grape? A region of production perhaps? Does it live up to the bouquet? Are the elements of the wine — acids, sugars, tannins, alcohol, wood, spice and fruit notes — in balance?

Four: Its finish in the throat. Is this a let-down? Or is it memorable and fully in keeping with the promise of the bouquet? Is it pleasant? Is it harsh?

Five: Is there anything left after you have spat it out or swallowed it? Is the wine lingering after it has disappeared? Or is it a flash in the pan? Of what is this mental sediment inspirational? The thought of a further glass? Or a ho-hum feeling of nothing special?

From this cosy sensory quintet, we are in a position to examine our feelings, our findings, more deeply. You can adhere to the above criteria — certainly I do at large tastings — and immediately feel in a position to evaluate the wine. I award it points out of 20 (but only after taking into consideration the wine's price as well). But we are not concerned with price, or points, here. We are concerned solely with the nature of the liquid in the glass. These five criteria can, after consideration, allow you to arrive at certain further judgements (or simply inspire purpler prose), all of utility for various reasons.

One: Does the wine have character? Or is it superficial? That is to say does it have, like an individual person, depth and fascination; or is it just a surface charmer? Are layers of flavour and texture discernible? Character implies depth, complexity, and a unclassifiable individuality. Such a wine will more readily inspire metaphor than it will easily find its place within the lexicon of conventional wine language. It may not be an expensive wine by any means.

Two: What is the real nature of its fruit? Is it typical? Does it have an element of real individuality? This has to do with how certain wines taste much like other wines and also, the obverse of this, how a wine might express its vineyard, region or wine maker's style. In a wine of true individuality, a certain singularity of aroma and taste is detectable. Perhaps even quirkiness. This is evidence of singular wine making and/or vineyard soil and climate which is unique.

Three:. Does the wine have an engaging texture? Can it be identified, or made analogous to, a material idea? Is it velvety? Is it silky?

Four: Is the wine elegant? Is it coarse?

Five: Is there a complexity above the norm? Does it have layers of flavour?

Six: Will the wine age, and develop more character and fascination over time? Certain aspects of the wine's tannin level, or acidity, or sugars, not to mention alcohol level, are enough to provide clues as to the wine's potential for development and exciting maturation over time. Often, it is the sum of these things which is the crucial factor. People often say to me, mildly protesting, 'Surely you only know if a wine will age with distinction once it has.' This is true, especially since natural corks always play so significant a part in variation between old bottles of the same wine of the same vineyard of the same year, as we saw in the previous chapter. But putting the lottery of the cork to one side, there are clues in the structure of the wine itself and these are broadly based on tannin, acidity, and sugar. Alcohol plays a part of course. Any drinkable young 10 per cent alcohol red wine, for example, would not be expected to age beyond a year or two, though many 9 per cent alcohol sweet wines last for decades.

Seven: What food might it most felicitously accompany? I hope this does not sound daunting but you must decide and discern for yourself — over time. If this area of wine tasting does seem to be a question of infinite response, I can only assure you that it will all become second nature with a little practice. As long as you care enough about it, you will crack it (not all wine writers have the marriage of food and wine sussed because they are lazy). This practice, unlike that at the cricket nets or in preparation for Grade Five piano, can be accomplished without monotony or pain and while you also pursuing other pleasures. Wine is a most convivial object of study and if your appetite for knowledge is large, your expertise will grow to match.

Drinking with our eyes

A good cook knows that we eat with our eyes as well as our mouths. It is a consideration of importance in all cultures. Americans insist food 'looks nice on the plate' and this has led to many vegetables being marketed which are flavourless yet visually magnificent (e.g. that jejune and uniquely US fruit, the toe-may-toe). The Japanese culinary appetite also regards presentation as important and turns a dish of food into a minor art form. Wine, considered properly, also contains intense visual pleasures. We digest it before we even put it into a glass, let alone our stomachs. That is to say, we see it on the shelf. Before we pour some wine and examine it, it is worth a small detour to consider the question of wine presentation and the nature of our perception of it. It is a factor of tasting. It is within our legitimate purview here. Sighted wine drinkers — and there are blind ones, hence the introduction of Braille-imprinted labels by the Rhône-based wine company Chapoutier — confront wine in two ways: in the bottle and in the glass. What does our sight tell us about a wine as it sits there, temptingly labelled or not, on a wine retailer's shelves?

The pleasure a well-designed label gives the eye and, importantly, how such a stuck-on advertisement promotes the wine's candidature for that dinner party at which, as host or hostess, we are anxious to impress, cannot be ignored. Most crucial here, for many ignorant snobs, is the insistence of the words on the label. Many a drinker is guided, persuaded and in the final analysis bludgeoned into believing in the sensory excellence of the wine within the bottle merely because the label says Château This or Domaine That. Lacking all taste (and the volition to develop it), such a wine buyer depends upon the sight of the label to convey what the wine within will often palpably lack on the taste-buds. This is foolish prejudice.

The image summoned up by the words on the label, and the shape of the bottle, can be extremely powerful. I have no doubt in my mind that the reason so many dry white wine drinkers cannot abide the idea of German wine is that the perception of such wine is of a hugely sweet confection and nothing else. This perception works in the same way that a sugar cube placed in the palm of your hand and shown to someone will immediately evoke sweetness in that person's mouth. A sweet sensation is created merely by the sight of the thing. No one is immune to this most human of all human phenomena (it would be wrong to call it a failing for it is a deeply buried instinct by which we preserve our ability to recognize what is good for us and what is bad). This is why so many of the new-fangled dry German wines come not in green Moselle or brown hock bottles, but in clear or light green bordeaux-shaped bottles. The eyes perceive these as presaging dryness.

Of all the sensory systems which appreciate the nuances of a wine, the eye is the most neglected. Yet we cannot help but look at a wine before we do anything else with it. The eye assumes its most important sensory role, once the wine has been poured. We drink with the eyes before we sip with the lips. This is one reason why a generous-bowled wine glass helps us appreciate wine the more. By inclining the glass to the horizontal we can, unless it is too full, form a half-moon reservoir of wine which brings us pleasure in contemplation.

It can be an immediate sensory experience, certainly for the experienced taster. A compelling colour in a wine glass, a lushly limpid gold or a meaty scarlet, is perceived by the pupil and the message taken to the brain, which cannot resist nudging the taste-buds via the saliva secretion glands, that greedier, more intense gratification is on the menu.

Often a polite glance is all that is permitted (at a professional tasting with 150 wines to get through, a polite glance is all the great majority of those wines would receive from me). The pleasure to be gained from regarding the colour of certain wines, however, is immense. Not only that, the sight of a wine and a scrutiny of it in the glass tell us much about it.

A wine glass is the wine taster's tool or the tosspot's bucket. Once you have become a taster of wine as well as a drinker of it and you have mastered the use of this tool, it will cease to matter where or when you taste or drink wine. It will become impossible for you to regard wine as anything other than an experience to explore every time you encounter it.

Less is more

One: Don't go over the top.
Whether you are experiencing wine at a tasting, responding to a *sommelier*'s first pouring, or drinking wine with food at home, it is always important that the glass can do its job properly. This means the wine must never reach the rim of the glass or even be within an inch of it; it must always be poured so that there is plenty of space to enable the wine to be agitated, spun, twirled, to dance in the glass without spilling. The wine must occupy no more than a quarter to a third of the glass. You cannot understand the nature of the wine if the glass is too full. The

glass as a tool, as a pleasure giver as much as an information provider, is blunted if there is too much wine within. You might just as well attempt to carve a neat wedge of Cheddar cheese with an adze as appreciate properly the wine in an overfull glass.

Two: Colour is full of meaning.

The colour of the wine as it moves within the glass is full of meaning. The white wine spectrum runs from the pale, almost watery hue of a recently released sauvignon or chenin blanc from the Cape (barely a few months old), through to the flaxen glint of eighteen-months-old chardonnay from California, to the fierce yellow of ten-year-old sauternes, to the burnt orchre/orange of a mature tokay. Red wine is no less poetic to the eye (although it does reserve its greatest complexities for the taste-buds) but its spectrum is denser and less reflective of polychromatic nuance: from the mournful blush-red of certain northern Italians through to the wishy-washy ruby of beaujolais, to the congealed blood of an Australian shiraz, to an ancient Madiran's pitch darkness relieved by patches of ripe damson purple. Rosé wines run from a blush-pink to an almost blood-orange hue.

Three: Describing the colour of a tomato.

How is it possible for any writer so to describe the colour of a fruit or a wine that the reader would immediately recognize it on sight? Certainly the crisp photographs within these pages help, but there is no eluding the fact that the true impact of a beautiful wine, or even an ugly one for that matter, is only caught *au naturel* when we eye it up in the glass. It doesn't help perhaps also to point out here that one person's perception of a colour is not necessarily the same as someone else's. What you call ruby I may term scarlet. We don't hear and see in the same way. Each impression enters a world known only to the individual who inhabits it. It is the same, maddeningly (yet delightfully for those who relish differentiation and distrust conformity), with all the faculties employed in wine tasting: sight, smell and taste. According to the philosopher's notion of 'perspectives', no rule can be held to be precisely true since every person perceives the reality of it from their unique angle of vision.

Four: The march of time.

We define and catalogue certain unalterable patterns within the colour of a wine. Lighter wine is younger wine; age brings depth (as can clearly be seen in the photographs). As you examine the wine in its circle of colour as viewed from above, two aspects become apparent. First, there is the denser colour in the middle of the wine. Second, there is the shading on the perimeter. This contrast shows us how the wine has aged.

Five: A clear clue (a).

A young wine can be almost as transparent as water at its edge. An old wine can show brown here, or a dark purple, an ochre or an orange hue. As you practise it over the years, experience will give you the eye to estimate accurately the age of the wine you are looking at. This skill is most readily seen in specialists of wines of a particular area, usually because they live and grow wine there, and thus regularly keep their faculties sharp, often infallibly so. No generalist wine drinker can hope to compete with such tasters.

Six: The right light.

When a wine is examined in decent light its history reveals itself. The traditionalist (and the romantic) will consider the light thrown by a candle to be best here, but the light thrown by a 60-watt spot against a white background is preferable. The age of the wine can be estimated better in such a light. In fact, candlelight is fairly useless when tasting wine, except, perhaps, for decanting.

Seven: A clear clue (b).

We can guess the approximate level of its alcohol from looking at a wine. By swirling the wine in the glass we not only release the bouquet of the fruit but also cause the wine to be drawn up the sides of the glass. As the liquid descends, it shows itself to be first, clear and uncoloured, and, second, to be trickling down in thin lines. More heavily alcoholic wines may create thicker trickles and more of them. The action of spinning the glass lightly in the hand centrifuges the alcohol which is denser and more volatile than the rest of the wine (which contains 70 per cent water in any case). As the wine is spun upwards, surface tension causes the wine immediately at the top of the glass to be drawn up the glass's sides and to adhere, there to stream back slowly in what some professionals term 'legs'.

The French call the phenomenon 'weeping'. The trickles are tears. In Germany, less poetically though no less fancifully, this phenomenon is sometimes called 'cathedral windows' because of the arc-like shape described by the returning wine; perhaps an unhelpful term since cathedral windows are rarely clear. But the alcohol is, and the more vivid the impression of the trickles, the greater the alcohol in the wine. Most wine you will encounter will be around

12 per cent but certain big reds reach 14 per cent or 15 per cent and of course fortified wine — port and some sherries — can be 18 to 20 per cent. Personally, I find that it is only when wine goes above 12 per cent alcohol that it forms significant tears although I have seen them form in semi-dry German wines of 9 per cent alcohol.

Not everyone, however, believes that the major constituent of these so-called legs is alcohol. I've heard even experts say that the clear liquid which is detached is glycerine (or glycerol — the terms, referring to a subtly sweet and thick chemical produced during a wine ferment, are interchangeable in this context). This view has been expressed to me by the odd German involved in wine, and even British wine personalities are attracted by the glycerine explanation. Michael Broadbent, who heads the auctioneers Christie's wine department, has written a book on wine tasting and even he, erudite as he is in wine matters, can't resist describing one wine as producing 'A noticeably heavy bead (legs) indicating high extract and glycerol', while elsewhere in the same book he writes that 'Full-bodied wines, those with high extract and alcohol content, form "legs" or "tears"…' He somewhat confuses the matter (and this reader) further when he adds that ' "legs" can also be created by the surface tension pump which is due to evaporation of the ethyl alcohol at the meniscus or rim'.

Poking around a charity bookshop I came across a copy of *The Essential Guide to Wine*, written by Robert Joseph and published by Tesco, and this states on page 47: 'Glycerine. The "fatty" constituent in some wines, making them taste richer — the "legs" which flow down inside the glass.' It may be that a natural confusion arises in non-scientific minds because glycerine is a clear liquid and decidedly viscous and also, of course, sweet. Thus not only is the eye deceived but also any tongue which, contriving to come into contact with a 'leg' or the 'legs' inside a whirled wine glass, would receive an impression (admittedly very subtle) of sweetness and viscosity.

However, alcohol is sweet too. The riper the grapes, the more glycerol in the wine. And it is also undoubtedly true, as Mr Broadbent asserts, that high alcohol, leading to the development of many 'tears' in a wine, is also a factor of 'high extract', to use his term. Therefore, in a ferociously honeyed and waxy pudding/blue cheese/foie gras wine, made from dehydrated grapes infected with the *botrytis cinerea* fungus where there is a high constituency of extracted chemicals, the level of glycerol can form the third biggest element after water and alcohol in the finished wine — that is to say, respectively, roughly 3 per cent glycerol, 70 per cent water and 14 per cent alcohol.

However, what remains a fact is that the 'legs' are alcohol. Perhaps the confusion arises because the higher alcohol necessary to show tears also indicates that the grapes were highly extracted and may well be rich in glycerol as a result. It is natural to wish that the evidence of one's own eyes must prove that what one is seeing can be explained logically, and in a way which adds to the expertise and analytical prowess of the seer. It is delicious to think that one can relate the phenomenon of 'legs' back to the grapes and how and when they might have been picked and from this deduce a sensory characteristic of the wine or judge its body. Only if body relates to alcohol level is this inference permissible. It is illuminating to point out here that it is the absence of a positive lexicon for wine terms, difficult to compile in so sensory and subjective a medium as wine tasting, which also adds to the confusion because 'body' to one taster is high alcohol whereas it is the richness which glycerol confers. This nagging linguistic imprecision among wine gurus illustrates, on top of everything else, that wine is never an absolute. Its very ineffability is, albeit charming, a trap.

Smell is the beginning of taste.

Five

5 The Well Connected Nose

(It's the only part of the brain open to persuasion)

'Invisible, intangible, indescribable — smells seem to defy reason.'
Ruth Scheps in 'Odeurs - l'essence d'un sens', *Autrement* review, Paris 1987

A simple experiment

Pinch your nose and smell the wine in your glass. Is it wine or could it be lemonade? You might never find out without your nose to guide you.

Now taste. Easy. It's lemonade. Now pinch your nose again. Are you still so sure it's lemonade? You cannot, by this token, effectively taste wine without smelling it. Even when the wine is in the mouth, the olfactory faculty is strongly operational and forms a significant part of the overall impression. Before we taste a wine, we cannot help but smell it first. ('Nosing it' is the tasting term.) To a wine taster, it is as impossible to omit smelling a wine before tasting it as it would be for a professional musician to forgo tuning his or her instrument prior to a performance.

It could be said, bearing this in mind, that wine tasting is a perverse pleasure in which the climax comes before the foreplay. In full-blooded wine drinking, this is often the case because the finish of the wine is not as uplifting and wonderful as the initial bouquet. This is why it is important when tasting a wine to permit it to register an impression in the back of the throat. If you were involved in a working day's tasting of, say, 120 wines, you would not want to swallow much of each one. If you did, you would be not only pickled but rendered incapable of exercising sane judgements. A short and happy life it would be for such a taster. It is, however, crucial that you gain an impression of the wine's finish in the throat.

Smelling the wine is all that is necessary to confirm its state of health. It is true that a wine might be sipped to ascertain other factors (whether it is chilled enough in the case of a white or whether it needs chilling in the case of a red served in warm weather), but the effect of the wine on the nose tells you everything you need to know about whether the wine is acceptable or not.

It is the esters and aldehydes — chemical compounds — that are largely responsible for the bouquet in wine. These change over the lifetime of a bottle and contribute to the rich charm of a great, developed wine, adding finesse and a multiplicity of sensational aromas. It is the membraneous nerves, minute receptor cells sited within the nasal cavities, that are responsible for catching an aroma, despatching its existence to the brain and setting in motion the reaction of pleasure or pain, of deliciousness or danger, that may result. At the same time as the thalamus awakens the memory bank of the studious drinker, a whole boxfile of information is mentally flicked through in seconds, revealing, perhaps, the wine's grape, its age, region of product, and even, in some of us, memories which have nothing whatsoever to do with wine *per se*. The smell of a wine is hugely evocative. The gastronome Brillat-Savarin, writing his magnificent *La Physiologie du goût (The Philospher in the Kitchen)* some time after the French Revolution (the book was published in 1825, a year before his death), remarked that 'I am . . . tempted to believe that smell and taste are in fact but a single sense,

whose laboratory is the mouth and whose chimney is the nose.' Later in the same book he refers to smell as 'that faithful sentry'. The nasal passage is an extension of the brain; indeed it can be said to be the only part of a human's cranial control centre exposed to the air.

What is true of the wine lover, and I would assume it also to be true of the enthusiast of chocolates, truffles or baked beans on toast, is that the introduction of certain smells to the nose not only stimulates the memory of an appetite but also plays a part in setting up the salivary glands to get out of bed and get ready for work, stimulating the taste-buds because at any second the mouth is going to need lubrication in order to soften the food to aid its digestion (not required in the case of wine, of course, but I don't suppose anyone has ever organized a palate to train its saliva glands to recognize wine as a liquid rather than a solid food before it touches the tongue). Thus, whatever we may think logically to the contrary, smell is taste. Or rather, it is the beginning of taste. It is taste leaping out of its starting-blocks but not yet in full stride. Jean-Anthelme Brillat-Savarin, fiddler, small-town politician, big eater, knew what he was talking about.

No extraneous smells, thank you

This may sound elementary, but you should avoid wearing perfumes or any kind of personal fragrance (aftershave is a real killer) when tasting wine. They are absolutely taboo, for obvious reasons. Also worth remembering is that if you wash your hands, during a toilet break perhaps, you should make sure you do not use strong soap and also that your hands are thoroughly rinsed. Perfume on an individual interferes with the bouquet of any wine in the vicinity, and the residue of soap on hands passes on an aroma to the wine glass as it is held which also affects the bouquet of the wine.

LA TECHNIQUE (but no la-di-da)

One: Agitating the glass forces up the aromas. The vaporization of the wine's esters, which form its aroma or bouquet, is encouraged by the movement of the wine and this enhances the impact of the esters on the nose by making them more concentrated. Pour just a little wine into the glass, so that you can really swirl it around without it spilling over the rim — or, for that matter, going up your nose when you inhale the bouquet.

Two: Don't breathe too exaggeratedly when you smell a wine. Breathe normally — inhale with a belly-stretching sniff not a snout-like intake of air. This does not, however, preclude taking as many of these inhalations as you like when a wine has an exquisite and multi-faceted bouquet.

Three: Take half the wine in the tasting glass into your mouth. If the glass is a large drinking vessel, take sufficient to feel the weight of the wine in your mouth but not so much that you cannot swish the wine around without gagging and swallowing. Close your lips, then purse them and suck in air. Get all the wine all around your mouth without letting any go down your throat yet. Let the air agitate the wine and enhance its impact on the taste-buds. The aeration the wine receives shows all its sides, good, bad, indifferent.

Four: I do not see how it is possible for a little wine not to trickle down the throat during tasting. This is important anyway, in my book, because you must get an accurate impression of how the wine will finish in the back of the throat, not just at the base of the tongue. You may, like myself at times, even tilt your head back to ensure your throat receives an impression of the wine.

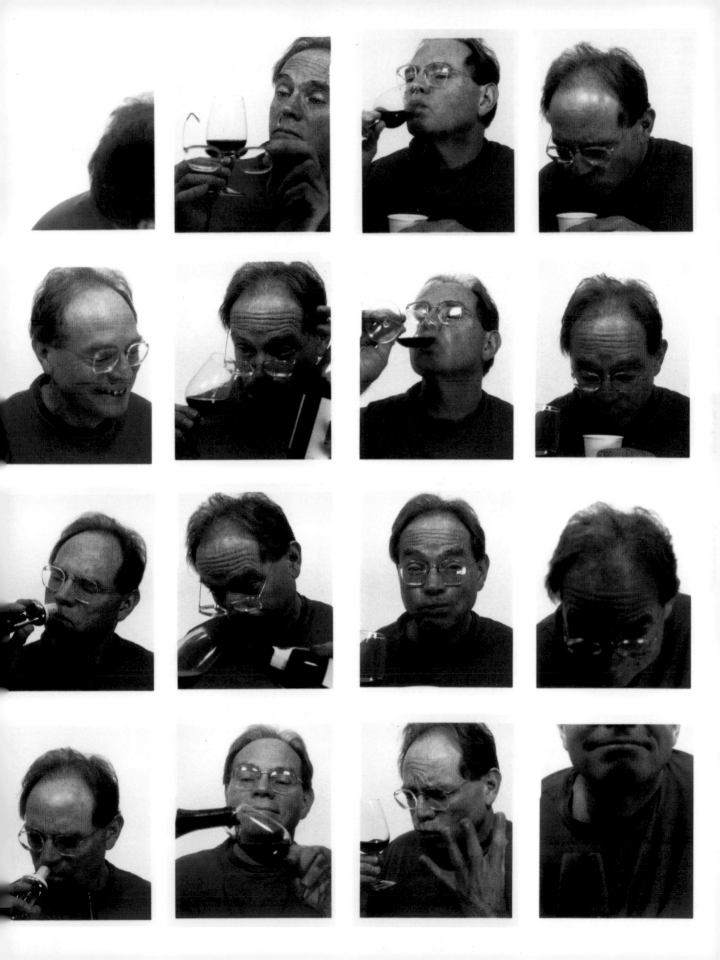

Five: Keeping your lips open to form a small 'O' shape, spit the wine out in an arc into a spittoon or bucket or sink. Sometimes I use a jug and simply empty it after every dozen or so wines. Do not slobber or spit half-heartedly. It is better if you do not incline your head too much as this encourages dribbling. Be firm with your lips; if you try to be overpolite or prissy the liquid projectile will splash all over the rim of the spittoon instead of neatly hitting its target. (One renowned wine writer is so inept at expectoration that his presence at a tasting ensures a stampede when he approaches the spittoon with bulging cheeks.)

Six: To practise all this, you can use water instead of wine. Once you know you can spin the water in the glass without spilling it, swill the water in the mouth without swallowing it, and spit it out without hitting other tasters or missing the target, you are ready for the real thing. Your clothes may become a little wet during this rehearsal, but they will not require dry-cleaning. Also, your outlay on wine is nil.

What can a nose detect? A personal classification of odours

I have long ceased to be surprised by the vast variety of smells and flavours even the greenest of tasters will discern in wine. Often, these are not simply show-offs but people who have genuinely been reminded of something, often personal, in a wine. In general, however, aromas and flavours are classified in groups we all recognize.

One: Wood. Normally, a skilled taster would only be able to distinguish French oak from American — Russian oak might be identified by a real specialist. Different forests confer subtly different odours and tastes, and there is a whole gamut of different tree smells which a uniquely gifted taster might detect.

Two: Fruit. How long is a piece of string? Normally, we sense melon, lemon, mango, strawberry, blackcurrant, blackberry, plum, prune, fig, pineapple, gooseberry, lime, apple, pear, lychee, passion-fruit, plus a few more, in wine. With scheurebe, the great unsung German grape, grapefruit is a key identifying mark.

Three: Flowers. This is a contentious area. Often, we merely say of a wine that it is 'floral'. This can range from the rich rosiness of a gewürztraminer to a faulty, geranium-smelling merlot. I know of no taster who has a catalogue of different flower smells at his or her disposal, any more than the rose aroma of that gewürztraminer is assigned to a specific variety of the flower. But the opportunity to develop the skill exists …

Four: Chemicals. Sulphur, hydrogen sulphide, acetone — these are the commonest. Petroleum is an important aspect of mature German rieslings; in the New World the tendency is towards paraffin. Both are deeply attractive traits and there could be hundreds of others. Plasticine is also a give-away aroma in certain German rieslings.

Five: Vegetables. Wow! We can run riot here. Green beans head the list (with certain cabernet sauvignons), then cabbage (faulty old white), carrots, cauliflowers, and a few others. But usually we simply refer to 'vegetality' in a wine.

Six: Herbs and Spices. Grass is a feature of certain sauvignons, coriander of some other whites. Tobacco is common as an aromatic element of anything from a Puglian peasant red to a pompous, cigar-boxy claret. Black pepper is not uncommon, sometimes cinnamon; once, I was convinced an Aussie chardonnay had cumin.

Seven: Is foxy a smell? It's pretty unpleasant. Gaminess, on the other hand (a feature of the finest pinot noirs) is rather an arousing aroma — some say erotic.

Eight: Fire. Burnt rubber can haunt the smell of a pinotage, smoke a sauvignon or chenin or even a verdelho. A roasted quality affects certain rich reds from warm climates.

Nine: Nuts. A general sort of nuttiness is a characteristic of several northern Italian whites made from many grape varieties. Chardonnay can exhibit a cob nuttiness. Sauvignon sometimes has a Brazil-nut edge. Almonds impinge deliciously on certain sherries. Coconut (a woody quality in truth) often infects riojas and is incorrectly inferred by some tasters to be a sign of the tempranillo grape. Sesame seeds can be a characteristic discernible in fine wines made from the viognier grape.

Ten: Foods. Butter is an indication of certain chardonnays. Oiliness is a characteristic of the same grape, too; semillon can also go that way. Coffee in cabernets, merlots and other rich reds is common; tea sometimes pops up in a merlot. Curry has been sighted in certain wines, but never by me. Chocolate is big in lots of reds.

What the nose can't spot

A gas chromatograph, lab machinery for defining the whole flavour breakdown of a wine, will show that a wine has scores of different smells and taste compounds. Even a great taster would be unlikely to discern more than a few. Indeed, I would say that anyone who attempted to develop human nasal detective powers to match those of a machine would be likely to end up bonkers — well, he'd be barmy even to try. Certain animals which depend upon their olfactory powers have a memory bank of 10,000 or more odours to call upon but no human can go quite this far, even though it is surprising how the average person may well be unaware of just how many hundreds of different smells, the various odours of everyday life, it would be possible to identify. It is pleasing to find complexity in a wine — this is the essence of a great wine — but to dwell on such things beyond any reasonable level of comprehension would be antisocial and aberrant. Carrying things to such a degree is an extreme most of us would consider excessive if not totally deranged; rather like the Middle Eastern Stylites who spent their lives atop pillars to be nearer God (an idea that originally developed merely to permit its saintly inventor to escape the pressing hordes of his devotees).

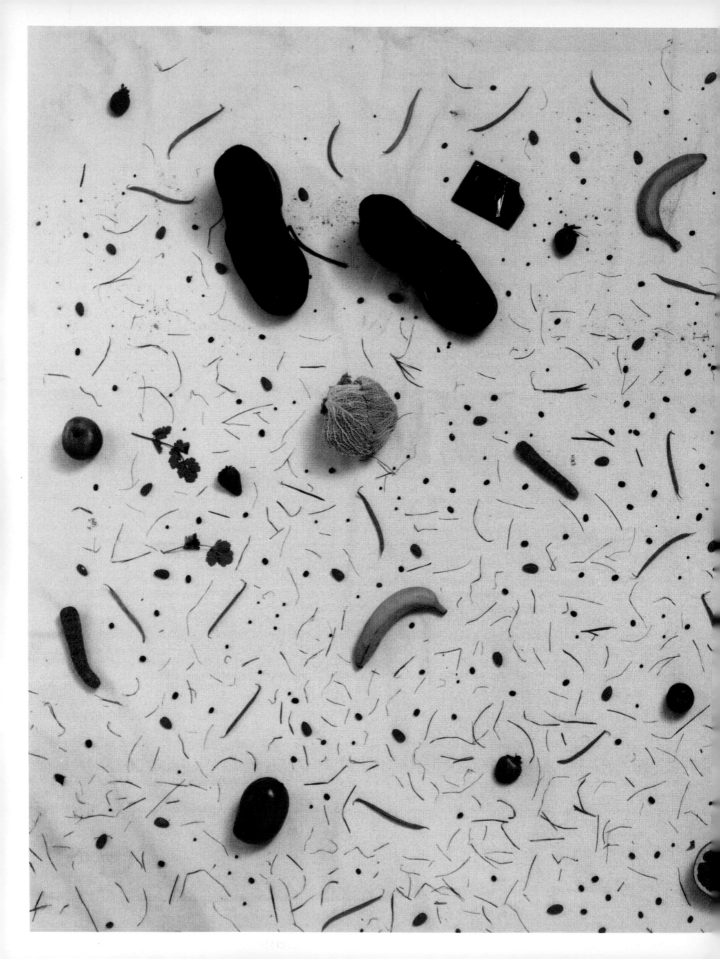

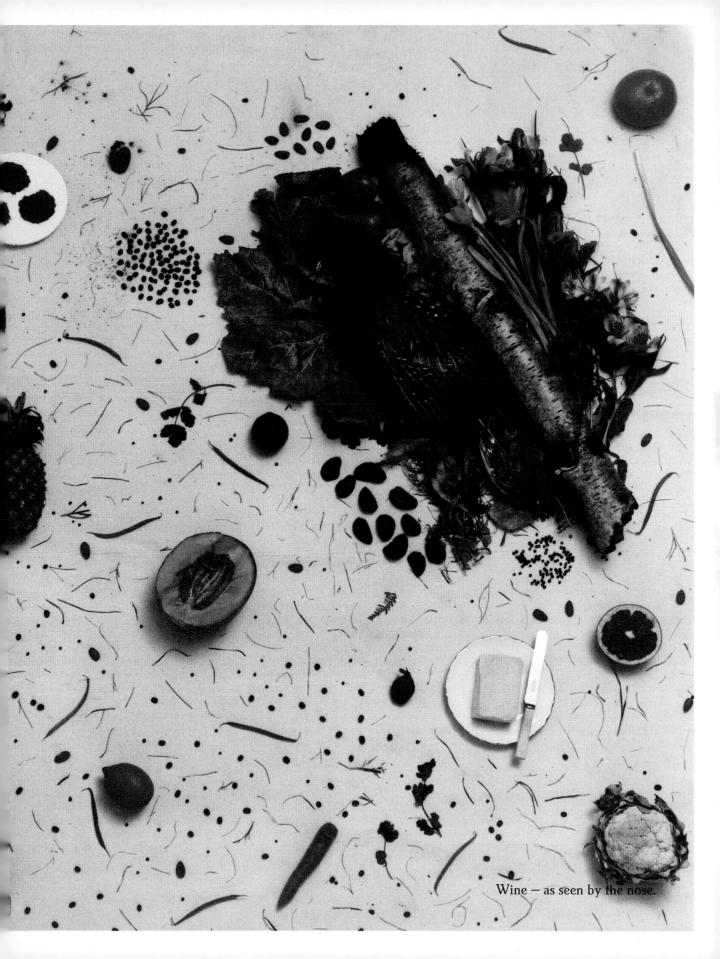

Wine — as seen by the nose.

The invention of the wheel

There has been an attempt to create a reliable vehicle for linguistically pigeon-holing the smell/taste spectrum of wine, and this is the Aroma Wheel devised by a professor of wine science at Davis University in California, Dr Ann Noble. Her wheel embraces, in three bands, 135 terms which can be applied to the sensory analysis of wine smells and their accurate identification. Thus fruity (as one primary band) leads to six secondary groups (citrus, berry, tree fruit, tropical fruit, dried fruit, other), which in turn lead to a tertiary band where, for example, citrus can mean either grapefruit or lemon, and dried fruit refer to strawberry jam, raisin, prune or fig. Some flavours are omitted — for example, there is no mango in the tropical fruit group (although the wheel I saw was of pre-1990 vintage and updated versions may contain this fruit, the flavour of which is sometimes to be discerned in the more exuberant Australian chardonnay/semillon blends).

What is being attempted here is a proper basis to enable professionals to agree on terms which can be applied intelligently and accurately to wines, with no sensible contradiction brooked. It is a brave, advanced and serious analytic terminological tool, the study of which is outside the scope of this book. It could be used in developing wine styles by wine companies where agreement on what a product actually does smell and/or taste like requires a consensus, and wine makers may have recourse to it. I know no wine writer who uses the wheel, but then Dr Noble may retort that there are so few genuine or scientifically oriented professionals in this field that to attempt to corral their terminology, often extravagant and highly personal, is outside her remit.

Wine writing is not tennis. A backhand volley is a precise and recognizable stroke which all players, spectators and commentators can agree on. On the Aroma Wheel, under the primary band entitled 'chemical' there is a secondary band labelled 'sulfur', leading to a tertiary band which includes the definition 'wet wool'. In my experience, this kind of smell is also reminiscent of certain dry young chenin blancs from the Loire where no sulphurous condition is the cause; it is in the nature of the style of the wine. What does one do? In my case, I can plead that's my personal reaction. In a winery laboratory or sales department, this would not be good enough. Dr Noble's wheel may have its uses in these circumstances.

Professor Noble approved the inclusion of her Wheel but wrote, not unreasonably, that 'I kinda don't like getting slammed as this write up does. Do I get rebuttal privileges?' The answer is indeed you do, professor. She goes on to point out that 'the wheel was not an attempt to pigeon hole, nor just for professionals. It is a LEXICON to guide people who are starting to try to describe wines so they can remember them better, to communicate them with others'. Anyone who is really serious about nailing down smells and flavours to be discovered in wines (on a fastidious scale beyond that attempted within these pages) would be well advised to access Professor Noble's website http://wineserver.ucdavis.edu//ACNoble//waw.html where a wealth of aromatics is opened up. The idea of using dried apricots to demonstrate the smell of sulphur dioxide, SO2, is especially inventive.

Featured opposite: Wine Aroma Wheel. Copyright A.C. Noble 1990.
Coloured laminated plastic copies of the wine aroma wheel are available from A.C. Noble, Dept. Viticulture and Enology, University of California, Davis, CA 95616, USA.
All proceeds support wine sensory research.
E mail: acnoble@ucdavis.edu

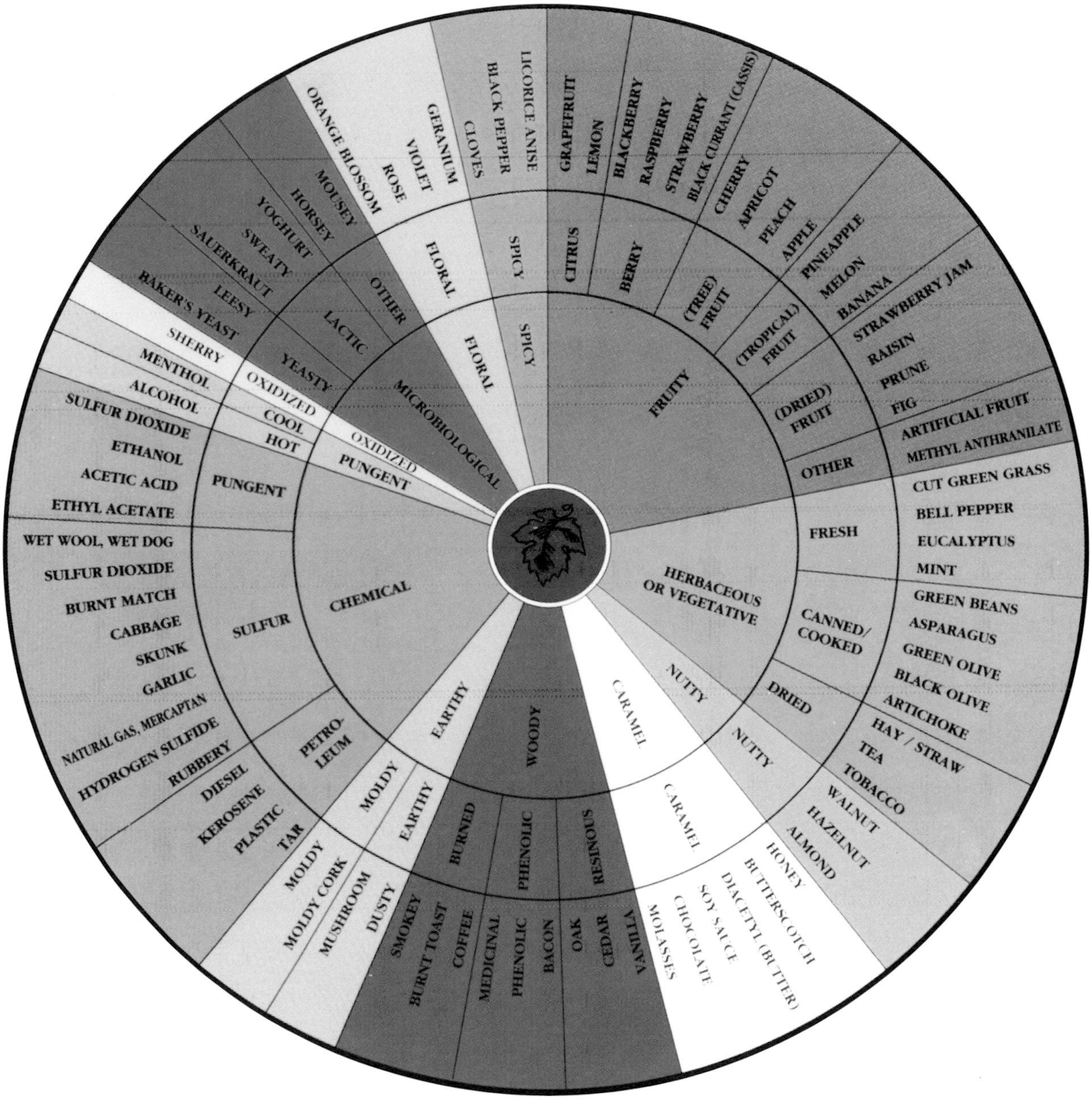

FRUITY
CITRUS
GRAPEFRUIT
LEMON
BERRY
BLACKBERRY
RASPBERRY
STRAWBERRY
BLACK CURRANT (CASSIS)
(TREE) FRUIT
CHERRY
APRICOT
PEACH
APPLE
(TROPICAL) FRUIT
PINEAPPLE
MELON
BANANA
(DRIED) FRUIT
STRAWBERRY JAM
RAISIN
PRUNE
FIG
OTHER
ARTIFICIAL FRUIT
METHYL ANTHRANILATE
HERBACEOUS OR VEGETATIVE
FRESH
CUT GREEN GRASS
BELL PEPPER
EUCALYPTUS
MINT
CANNED/ COOKED
GREEN BEANS
ASPARAGUS
GREEN OLIVE
BLACK OLIVE
ARTICHOKE
DRIED
HAY / STRAW
TEA
TOBACCO
NUTTY
NUTTY
WALNUT
HAZELNUT
ALMOND
CARAMEL
CARAMEL
HONEY
BUTTERSCOTCH
DIACETYL (BUTTER)
SOY SAUCE
CHOCOLATE
MOLASSES
WOODY
RESINOUS
OAK
CEDAR
VANILLA
PHENOLIC
MEDICINAL
PHENOLIC
BACON
BURNED
SMOKEY
BURNT TOAST
COFFEE
EARTHY
EARTHY
MOLDY
MOLDY
MOLDY CORK
MUSHROOM
DUSTY
CHEMICAL
PETRO-LEUM
DIESEL
KEROSENE
PLASTIC
TAR
SULFUR
WET WOOL, WET DOG
SULFUR DIOXIDE
BURNT MATCH
CABBAGE
SKUNK
GARLIC
NATURAL GAS, MERCAPTAN
HYDROGEN SULFIDE
RUBBERY
PUNGENT
PUNGENT
ETHYL ACETATE
ACETIC ACID
ETHANOL
SULFUR DIOXIDE
HOT
ALCOHOL
COOL
MENTHOL
OXIDIZED
OXIDIZED
SHERRY
MICROBIOLOGICAL
YEASTY
BAKER'S YEAST
LEESY
LACTIC
SAUERKRAUT
SWEATY
YOGHURT
OTHER
HORSEY
MOUSEY
FLORAL
FLORAL
ORANGE BLOSSOM
ROSE
VIOLET
GERANIUM
SPICY
SPICY
CLOVES
BLACK PEPPER
LICORICE ANISE

Where wine is concerned, the sexes are not equal.

Why do women have the nose for wine and men the guts?

Women have more enhanced olfactory faculties. Men have a greater propensity to absorb alcohol successfully.

These two assertions are more than the mere speculative fancies they were once considered to be. They now have some scientific buttressing.

Women have a greater inbuilt need (and thus ability) than men to recognize, discern, appreciate and collate smells, odours and perfumes. This is a generalization, of course, because women are not uniquely gifted — some men can, by making the effort, become their equals, but they have to make the effort; women, in general, have a naturally enhanced sense of smell. Why?

It would seem to be a deeply etched racial mechanism whose origins can be theoretically traced to the need for the less aggressive help-meet of the hunter-gatherer to acquire the full range of defensive skills necessary for survival. One of these would have been to develop the nose as a means of recognizing differences in fruits, herbs, animals: of identifying the contents (and most importantly any feral inhabitants) of dark caves; of recognizing people, even, perhaps, of distinguishing one child from another. The male, flexing new found muscles and broadening his bellicose instincts, developed more physical attributes. It is possible that both female and male were born with equally fine olfactory faculties but the male's became less acute through emphasizing the more physical aspects of appetite and the senses. Desensitizing perhaps begins with losing an appreciation of aromatic nuances.

Was, then, the Mesopotamian who developed — some 5,000 years ago it is said — the distillation process which extracts perfumes from flowers and plants (thus also providing us with the word alcohol, from the Arabic *al-kuhl**) a woman? What is beyond argument is that somewhere along the line women developed their interest in aromas and this eventually resulted in the modern cosmetic industry where thousands of perfumes are on sale — and many women can not only distinguish one smell from a score of others but have habitual recourse to a range of scents and eaux-de-toilette for a variety of uses, times of day and moods. If smell was not so central to human experience, the world would be so much less of an experience; you hardly need to be an aromatherapist or even a chef to appreciate that. Such complexities, such niceties of purpose, are often lost on a man. He can, however, as compensation for this lack of finesse, drown his disappointment.

He can drink more. How? Why?

Women have smaller livers for a start, and so have fewer alcohol-degrading enzymes available. Alcohol is also absorbed into the bloodstream differently in a woman. Women, it seems, lack an enzyme men take (unknowingly) for granted: alcohol dehydrogenase. This inhibits the stomach and deconstructs alcohol when it reaches the gut, so less alcohol, less quickly, goes into the male bloodstream. There are also differences in body weight and water content between men and women which contribute to a man's ability to absorb more booze without feeling its adverse effects as quickly as a woman.

Indeed, the latest research from Finnish researchers has concluded that alcohol raises ovarian testosterone levels in women but has no effect on that hormone's levels in men when alcohol

* *Al-kuhl* means kohl, the blue dye derived from antimony which has over the centuries stained many an odalisque's eyelids a more alluring hue.

is absorbed. Admittedly, the research base of fifty women and fifty men is very small but the findings are noteworthy. If testosterone, the male sex hormone, is increased in a woman's body under the stimulation of alcohol, then the aphrodisical reputation of certain drinks, especially sparkling wine with its enhanced speed of entry into the bloodstream due to its gas, is not based on myth. Wine makes women randier, that's what the Finns are claiming.

I have also received anecdotal evidence that women who drink to excess — hardly within this book's remit but worth mentioning in passing — are, unlike men who similarly abuse alcohol, apparently more prone to guilt-ridden hangovers and depressive moods. I can offer the evidence of one male here: 'I have never felt guilty or depressed, even with a (rare) whopping hangover, and I never say "I'll never drink that much again".' Women, in my experience at least, are more sensible in this regard. They say 'How stupid of me!' and then swear they'll never touch another drop. It's a woman's nature to be so; and, as the nineteenth-century prelate Sydney Smith's precociously sage young son once remarked, 'Nature . . . is only another word for mystery; it only means that we know nothing at all about the matter.'

Mood changes with wine are, however, a blessing bestowed on both male and female drinkers. Isn't this why we enjoy wine? No one needs to get roaring drunk or even gauchely merry to appreciate this. Music also changes our moods. Wine with music can be a catharsis. Once, in the foulest of foul tempers and even feeling a trifle sickly, I stuck on the earphones and listened to something soothing while quaffing a generous quantity of Chilean cabernet sauvignon and I was transformed within five minutes into a placid, well-feeling individual.

A bar of chocolate works the same trick with some people. Theobromine, a bitter alkaloid found in the cacao tree's seeds, is one of the stimulating chemical constituents found in chocolate. There are happy foods, there are sad foods. In a biblical life-span of seventy years, the average European will consume between 30 and 40 tons of food and, if so minded, a considerable gallonage of wine. A French wine drinker, for example, appetite-active between the ages of twenty and eighty, let us say, and consuming the estimated annual per capita amount, will get through 3840 litres of wine in that lifetime, the average Brit on the bottle, around 720 litres. My estimate for my own consumption if I live that long is 12,500 litres, as it happens. How is it possible for such consumption, with all of us, not to have a massive influence on the moods created through the central nervous system's reactions to all the chemicals contained in all that food and drink? We are what we consume. Apart from the proven beneficial health implications of wine drinking, there are possibly many other aspects of the individual wine drinker's personality which derive from the habit. Wine drinking makes for happy, optimistic humans.

Where women are concerned, pregnancy also makes an impact on the faculties of taste and smell. Hormonal changes take place (as early as six weeks in) which can affect the sense of smell and taste; most important, I believe, is the change when motherhood fully arrives. The craving for certain tastes before the birth is carried on via a broadened ability to detect and recognize odours and tastes which directly affect the mothering of the child and this may — and I say 'may' for this is a hunch, barely an informed speculation — enhance the olfactory skills of the female wine taster even further.

In order to become the most accomplished wine tasters, then, do men need to acquire certain specific feminine characteristics?

Very probably. Almost certainly. Not good news for the old-school-tie brigade, is it?

Six

6 Anyone Can Have an Off-Day

(The different and often maddening aspects of taste)

First: When to taste?

Wine is different at different times (of the day, of the year, of your life). The wine you taste at 11.30 a.m. will not be the same wine if you taste it at 3.30 p.m. having eaten lunch. There are optimum times to taste wine, when the palate is at its sharpest and most appreciative. For me this is any time between ten in the morning and three in the afternoon, nothing being eaten meanwhile; and, apart from this, in certain circumstances (where only a small set of wines is to be tasted) between five and eight in the evening, before dinner, and not after any sort of tea or spicy or alcoholic lunch has been consumed.

I am of the unshakeable opinion that to taste wines — and I mean here a range of several wines, not merely one or two — when the faculties of the taster are at their height involves choosing a time before any large meal is consumed. This (for me at least) also includes breakfast. Mostly I only eat fruit for breakfast, rarely anything more, and even when I do eat a breakfast treat of kippers I would never do so knowing I was going to be tasting a range of wines that day. The only exception is when I am travelling and tasting many wines at different retailers over a concentrated period of several weeks and then it is my habit, if I am tasting 100 wines at one retailer in the morning and the same number or more at another retailer in the afternoon, to have a small cooked breakfast and skip lunch altogether.

An experiment worth trying would be to ask a group of tasters to rate and describe a set of a dozen or so wines, then offer them a substantial lunch, and then present them with the same wines, disguised or otherwise made anonymous, to taste and analyse. I think it would be reasonable to expect any truly great wine, and perhaps any really rich red or fortified wine, to make its greatness manifest in either circumstance, but many interesting wines of middling complexity and merit, especially delicate whites, would fare less well, seem less convincing and concentrated in fruit, in the afternoon session.

It is not only food that comes between the taster and a wine, it is also the time of day itself. The taster — I cannot stress this point too much — is at his or her most receptive during the morning/pre-lunch period. An evening session is not precluded but it has to feature a short flight of wines. In any event, the evening session is not an unusual professional gathering, often connected with an ambitious dinner (after a discreet tasting) when the wines are matched with certain dishes. Sales-hungry wine merchants also often put on tastings for their richer customers in the evenings and even though by then most people's clock is beginning to run down, such tastings are often a spur to appetite (and to buying wine). But an evening tasting requiring hours of scrutiny and reflection, featuring many scores of wines of all styles, is a rarity.

At professional tastings of several styles of wine, the most I can comfortably manage in an early evening session is thirty bottles. However, I often feel that a wine considered somewhat dullish in an evening session might fare rather better in a morning one, when eager-to-learn palates would be sharper and more receptive to nuance. Mood is also an obstacle to wine appreciation and accurate evaluation. This may involve tiredness at an inappropriate time of day or it might be connected with the taster's frame of mind. I cannot, for example, see how anyone could offer a sensible analysis of a wine when in a towering rage or, for that matter, distracted by other preoccupying thoughts.

The professional taster who does the job regularly must needs be aware of such considerations. I have twice in my career pulled out of attending tastings because I considered I was in such a filthy humour I would be unable to taste properly. This is rare and only of passing interest.

Second: Everything, including wine, tastes different at different temperatures

The temperature at which we drink a wine is crucial to the degree of pleasure that wine will provide. Don't we all know this? Who sips warm champagne or iced shiraz? No doubt somebody does, somewhere, and we can't deny that person his right, having bought the bottle, to do as his appetite dictates. But such extremes of temperature are hardly indulged in by the pleasure seeker with a normal temperament.

The age-old rule dictates that white wines are drunk chilled, red wines at room temperature. But... what is chilled? And can you tell me what room temperature is? Two more imprecise and misunderstood shibboleths of wine lore, as parroted by the wine bore, do not exist.

One: Chilled does not mean cold. It does not mean icy. It does not mean freezing. It means the equivalent, I reckon, if the season is a cool one, of forty minutes in a refrigerator which is not turned up to maximum. In summer, it means perhaps an hour.

Two: What wine? The white wine to be chilled according to the notion above is anything in the chardonnay, sauvignon blanc, dry chenin blanc, pinot gris or grigio, viognier, semillon, New World riesling, etc. line-up. The exception I would make is for dry, kabinett, or spätlese level German or Alsatian rieslings, the demi-sec Loire whites (Vouvray, Coteaux du Layon, Bonnezeaux, etc.) and any of the dry and off-dry traminer grapes (from New or Old World); here I think thirty minutes' cooling is sufficient even in summer. Riesling is a delicate little beast in spite of its legendary longevity in the bottle, the acidity is paramount with it, and if the wine is too cold the fruit is numbed and the balance less than perfect — though this is a perception rather than a reality since it is the taste-buds which are confused in that they sense the sharpness of the acidity over the sweetness of the fruit. I think the same is true also of off-dry Loire chenin blancs. When the temperature of such a wine is at its nicely and lightly chilled optimum, so is the wine.

Three: Sweetness and temperature. Sweeter German wines, and the sweet dessert styles of wines like sauternes or monbazillac should be chilled longer as with normal table wines. These guide-lines apply for drinking wine in a relaxed situation as well as for formal tasting situations.

Four: An indistinct chill. I haven't given a precise temperature in this section because I don't know anyone who bothers to test for such a thing in a wine even though wine manuals always tell you such-and-such a degree is the right one at which to serve wine. Can you tell me how to tell the temperature of a wine without going to a great deal of trouble? Do you insert a needle-thermometer through the cork? Or what? Is there some kind of fancy apparatus which can gauge wine temperature through the glass of the bottle? Pshaw, I say. You'll have to make do with my fridge rule of thumb. I can't be doing with wine thermometers, finicky gimmicks.

Five: Bubbles. With sparkling wines, a simple generality: cool them for one hour and one hour fifteen minutes at most. No longer; unless the refrigerator is on a very low setting indeed.

Six: Red wines. Where red wines are concerned and the sacred 'room temperature' beast rears its head, it needs to be understood that this phrase was coined in an era of drinking when

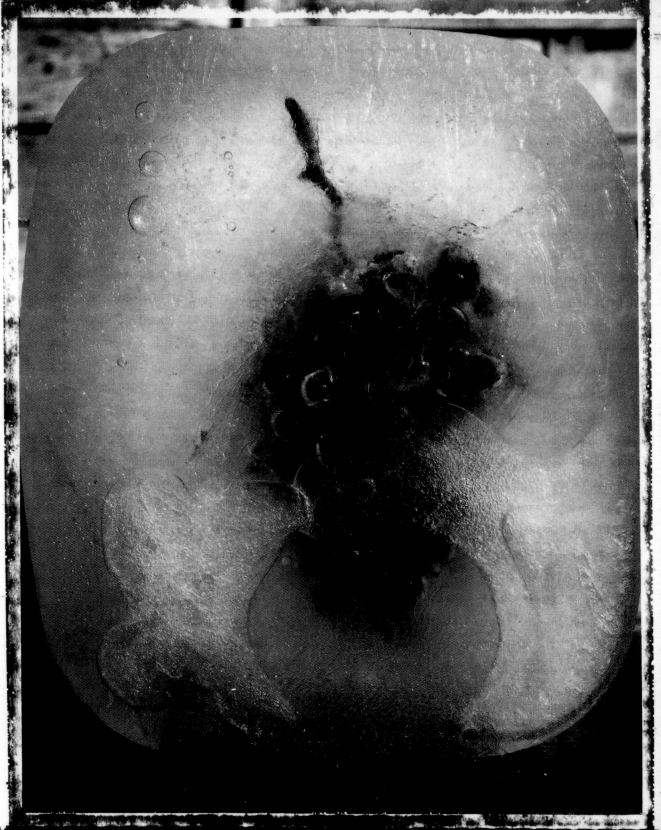

wine was habitually brought up out of cellars, not hoisted out of supermarket trolleys, and the temperature of the bottles was correspondingly low. In a proper cellar such wines would have maintained an even temperature and any white brought up from it would be at drinking temperature without the need for further cooling, though this was doubtless done anyway, especially with sparkling wine and hock, which went into the ritual silver bucket filled with ice. The wine also went into a room which was not centrally heated, notwithstanding the presence, perhaps, of a blazing fire, and certainly with the popularity in those days of highly tannic clarets getting on in years, drinking them cool would have been an abomination. Hence the rule that any red wine to be served at dinner must be brought up by the butler from the cellar at lunchtime or even in the morning so it could chambrer (from the French and meaning to bring to room temperature). This is as far as the wine law under review at the moment can take us. If you have open fires, a butler and a cellar, make use of them as you will.

Seven: Room temperature. Red wine served at room temperature simply means the wine has stood in its bottle for several hours in a room heated to between 60 and 70°F (21°C max). Although not every red wine appreciates such mollycoddling warmth, a tannic example does need some warmth, even in summer; thus, young to middle-aged Bordeaux, Rhônes, the heavier Spaniards (prioratos, riojas), chianti classicos, barolos, the bigger Aussie cabernets and shirazes, and certain South African (cabernets), Californian (zinfandels), New Zealand (merlots and cabernets), Chilean, Argentinian and Portuguese reds (have I left anyone out? Oh yes, the Lebanese Château Musar), are happier served, to my mind, around 66°F (18°C). Personally, I actually go for the lower of these two if I can manipulate things, which is not easy if all you want to do is sit back and relax and let the wine simply flow soul-warmingly through you.

Eight: Hot weather. Wines made from the pinot noir grape — gamay, inexpensive pinotage, grenache, young non-classico chiantis, valpolicellas and north-eastern Italian reds generally, young Spaniards, Chilean merlots, South Africans cinsaults, Australian generic reds, and so on — then I like the wine definitely cool most of the time. When the weather is sultry or hot, especially when the weather is humid and it's mid-summer madness time, cooling such wines to almost a chilled state is, to my taste, essential.

Nine: Humidity. Mature pinots are better slightly warmer as are the bigger, hairy, richer pinotages, but I'd always serve other New World pinots lightly chilled in summer (half an hour in the fridge) and certainly the light-style Italians. Red wine in warm and humid conditions tastes more alcoholic because the alcohol is evaporating and it overwhelms the fruit, being so reactive to the heat. I have tasted red wines at room temperature on a humid afternoon and it was like sucking on a rasp; next day, at ten in the morning, newly opened bottles of the same wines were as smooth as the velvet their makers intended them to be.

Ten: Rosés. Rosé wines, like sherries, are best served under 50°F (10°C) (if you must have a temperature figure). Fortified wines around 20 to 25 per cent alcohol are better chilled, unless they are big and rich, like port, when they can, in winter certainly, be served like red wine. In summer, however, even great port appreciates cooling its heel.

Eleven: Port. Generally, this is served, like red wine, at the temperature to which its prevailing surroundings can bring it; yet I was once served a geriatric vintage port at a shipper's house on the Douro in a decanter with a fine mist of condensation on it — straight from the fridge where it had been kept — but then the temperature outside on the patio was 112°F (44°C). Personally, I thought the port too cold, and the wrong drink to have anyway with such exterior heat, though tawny port is certainly pleasant chilled on a warm day.

Twelve: Chilling idea. There is one other idea you can resort to, although in my experience the only people who do it are certain bar personnel in the warmer of the United States and champagne waiters in France. One of the most refreshing experiences of civilized living is to drop in on some roadside tavern on a hot Californian afternoon and see your beer, cool from the tap, being poured into a glass already icy from a special fridge. It is a lot of trouble to go to, chilling glasses, but in certain circumstances it can be intensely civilised.

Thirteen: Changing times, changing climes. Overall, people serving wines at even quite august assemblies often fail to pay attention to the temperature of the bottles when only a small degree of the consideration given to the food in this regard, which no one would dream of serving cold if it was supposed to be hot or luke-warm, would suffice. True, it is a little extra trouble to go to. But then anyone reading this book is obviously prepared to go to reasonable lengths to enjoy wine anyway, so getting the temperature right is a trifling discipline.

As with wine, so it is with food. There was a time when to offer a Briton a cold soup would be to risk having it thrown in the cook's face. Soup was broth. It was always served hot. But since our embracing of chilled vichysoisse, who has not enjoyed iced cucumber soup? Or gazpacho? Or a dozen other chilled yet savoury liquids?

With all that sun-spot activity turning southern Britain into a sub-Mediterranean climate at certain times of the year, perhaps the fashion for chilled wine will become more widespread. I, for one, very much hope so.

Third. A matter of Highs and Lows. But is it the state of the weather or the mood of the taster?

There is a factor which can affect the taste of wine which receives no notice whatsoever. This is the weather at the time of drinking. This is not connected with the level of the temperature but to do with air-pressure systems, or cyclonic activity. I have no scientific evidence for this assertion but I do have the concurrence of a few professional wine tasters.

Some of them agree with me that:
One: When there is a high-pressure system, that is to say, the sun is out and the sky is blue, any wine's smell and taste seems lifted and more noticeable.
Two: Low-pressure conditions, drizzly and cloudy, numb the wine — any wine. Wines of extremes — big tannic wines and taut, unwooded whites — seem less well defined.
Three: Now. The Big Questions. Do weather fronts genuinely affect the smell and taste of wine? Or are these effects within the taster rather than the wine?

Baby vines in the warm Cape.

Meteorologists with cold feet

I can find no meteorologist who will do anything more than nod and say 'Sounds reasonable' to the weather-front question. But then we all know how we feel within ourselves when the weather's great or the weather's rotten, so who's to say it isn't our feelings that affect the performance of the wine?

Moot point here. And I've got nowhere trying to acquire hard scientific evidence that weather has a dramatic effect on the organoleptic peformance of a wine — that is say, how it impacts on human organs of smell and taste — either by affecting its chemical constituents or by dulling the metabolism of the drinker. Certainly, as any wine maker will testify, weather affects wine in other ways. I have seen for myself the agitation caused in newly bottled St-Emilion of the previous year's vintage when a thunderous weather front gathered itself, 300

Mature specimens in cold wintry Surrey.

or 400 miles out to sea. I have also witnessed, at various seasons of the year, the effect on young wine of the growth cycle of the vines it came from and how, in the *vigneron*'s words, 'The young wine seems to mirror, by its clarity and appearance in bottle, the development of the vines which gave it birth.'

No visitor to Beaujolais in the old days failed to return without his ears ringing with the mystical pronouncements of certain growers to the effect that 'One must never try to bottle the wine when the moon is on the wane and the wind is in the north' — or was it the south?

We might take pause for consideration before we pour scorn on such gypsy sounding folklore. The moon and the sun create tides and much else besides. Their effect on wine, with its myriad metallic trace elements, must have some magnetic connection.

The case for mood

Wine can make us happy. We can all agree on that. But can our mood change our response to a wine? There may be more than just dispositional factors at work here. There may be bodily chemical ones.

I am compelled to make this perhaps richly contentious statement because of the evidence on human feelings and health published by the Association for Research into the Science of Enjoyment, an enterprise founded by a professor at Reading University, David Warburton. Studies by this Association measured the effects that good and bad experiences had on the body's stimulus to produce the antibody immunoglobulin. This is found in saliva, as a defence against respiratory infections. Happy thoughts, the research demonstrated, increased the amounts of the immunoglobulin produced; unpleasant thoughts, the reverse. Does this not suggest, therefore, that the happy taster's saliva is chemically different from the sad or disappointed taster's saliva?

In other words, our disposition, our mood, as we taste a wine may create chemical conditions in the body which may alter the way that wine tastes. I am given cause to wonder, in the light of Professor Warburton's profound research, if I am, after all, the right person to be pontificating on wine tasting. I rarely taste wine in any other state but an extremely happy one. Perhaps I should try tasting when I'm in the foulest possible mood so that I can reach a more balanced judgement.

Wine retailers with cold feet but with warm hearts

Now it must be said here that when I contacted, via letters, certain wine buyers at supermarkets and high street wine shops about the matter of wine and weather, none felt moved to reply in romantic mode. I got the distinct impression that some of them felt they didn't wish to commit themselves in writing (to a crank, what's more) on such an ill-researched and arguable subject.

The only buyer who did respond immediately, by fax, was Mr Steve Daniel of Oddbins (no cold feet here). He wrote: 'I'm afraid I can't add much on the scientific front. However, as you know I really do believe that air pressure does have an effect on how the wines taste. It is exactly as you say: high pressure and the wine tastes fruitier and more expressive. Low-pressure wines become dumb and reticent.'

Mrs Elizabeth Robertson, who heads Safeway's wine-buying team, responded with a more cautious 'Wines do taste different at different times and there doesn't always seem a clear reason for it.' She went on: 'There are a multiplicity of factors here and surely air pressure is only one part of it. There are times when such and such a wine tastes brilliant and another time when the wine is as dull as dull can be. Is there a waxing and waning mood implied in the taster perhaps?'

This point was also picked up by Mr Robin Tapper, who manages Sainsbury's wine-buying department. He is also a geographer and so I was keen to receive what I hoped might be a brief insight into the subject but he was content to equivocate between the two imponderables: is it the weather affecting the wine or the taster being affected by the weather? He felt unable to come down strongly on either side, though he did agree that wine was different at different times and weather conditions played a part in this.

Over the past few years, as I have become convinced that wine reacts to the weather not only as a fermenting liquid or when maturing in a barrel but as bottled artefact, I have tried out my theories on wine buyers and wine makers but never received a scientific explanation for the phenomenon. When I talked to three wine makers based in France on the subject — Thierry Boudinaud who is based in the Rhône, and Nerida Abbott and Nigel Sneyd, a pair of brave Aussies who are attempting to revolutionize beaujolais (hallelujah!) — I received much sympathy but no hint as to what might be happening to create differences in the same wine on different days.

Nerida: 'It could be the moon. We all know convection currents and lunar movement affect the wine in the tank. Pressure systems have an influence on the wine when it's fermenting.' Thierry: 'We do the racking of the wine when the mistral's blowing. The wine is clearer. The lees stay at the bottom. So yes, the weather affects the wine in that way.' But does it affect the taster? He shrugged. Maybe yes, maybe no. (Racking is the winery process where the clean, fully fermented wine is taken out of tank or barrel, and the lees, the gunge of pips and skins and bits of unresolved pulp which contribute flavour, complexity and various chemical elements to the wine, go to the bottom. Racking can happen once or twice a year with barrel-aged wine; perhaps less often in some areas. The lees form the marc or pomace which can be spread on the vineyard as nutrient for the soil or be distilled into such things as marc de bourgogne or marc de champagne.)

Flight of fancy?

It is true, of course, that air pressure affects wine on aircraft and British Airways is only one of several airlines which selects wine on the basis that certain examples have characteristics, a more obvious fruitiness, which make them expressive and fluent 6 miles high in a pressurized air cabin. But in the airline situation there is the obvious difference that height makes to the taster where dehydration, humidity, stale recycled air and measurable differences in oxygen quality create an effect on the nose and the mouth and the throat. It seems reasonable here to come down on the side of the taster, not the wine, and put the reasons for any wine to taste as it does in the sky firmly at the door of the nasal passages and palate. But on the ground we are not aware of these changes in our physical make-up. On the ground we are surely in an optimum state to taste wine and if there are differences in our metabolism which might affect the taste of wine then they must be minimal.

Feet on the ground

Which is where we must let Nigel Sneyd have the last word. He put his case strongly: 'There is no logical or scientific reason why a wine opened in warm weather should taste different from the same wine opened when it is raining.' Then he thought for a bit and added: 'Physiologically, it may be all to do with how the nose works in dry, warm conditions compared to how it works when it's colder or overcast.'

Good point. However, what came next was not such an inviting notion. 'I think,' he said slowly, 'if it is all to do with air pressure as you say then you should taste some wine at ground level then take the wine down in a diving bell. Taste the difference, if any, for yourself. Only way to do it.'

I thank Nigel for this brilliant idea. However, as a person who cannot tolerate confined spaces for longer than a few minutes, I would never survive the trip down let alone the trip back up — even if I had a bottle of fine old Alsatian riesling with me as both test-bed and fortification.

Maybe Mr Sneyd was trying to tell me something.

Seven

7 The Crucial Clues

(Name that grape!)

We enter here a stormy and somewhat contentious area of wine tasting. What does a grape smell and taste of to such a neat and classifiable extent that its identity is immediately apparent? The answer is nothing and everything.

Nowadays wine is like literature, cooking, clothes, music, and even shampoo — broad in scope, multi-faceted in definition, deep in style and wide in provenance. Gone are the days, only a generation ago, when half-a-dozen grapes from half-a-dozen countries constituted all that most wine drinkers, and candidates for any master of wine exam, needed to acquaint themselves with, and the world is all the more exciting for such cosmopolitanization.

There are some 4000 grape varieties from which wine can be made. Only 1 per cent need detain us here. That is, twenty red and twenty white. It is a purely arbitrary pairing of numbers on my part. I had to stop somewhere and even though a variety like palomino is absent, is it any loss, categorically speaking? It makes sherry and is only worth discussing, to my mind, in this highly evolved form; as an unfortified table wine palomino makes an utterly anonymous liquid of little interest or varietal fascination. My list is, then, selective and chosen on the basis of the international usage of the varieties. These are the grapes you will see most often on a wine label.

The top forty

So forty varieties it is. Dare I pin words to each to describe their smell/taste sensations? It is a foolhardy venture, one fraught with risk, contradiction, and next year's vintage (which may, for a certain variety in a certain region, change everything). Well, can it be achieved by relating each variety to a region where it is grown and defining it further? This is certainly a necessary extension even if it is only in the form of an added notation. A grape variety from one part of the world may have less in common with the same variety from another part than do two different varieties from the same region. Yet even here no generalization works every time with every variety, just as it wouldn't if applied to people. You could also further leaven this complex, self-raising loaf by mixing in vintage variation and any wood influence, but by this time you would have too lengthy an analytic process to make the definitions of any use.

But there is a nebulous consensus about the flavours of certain grapes. What follows reflects this, along with my own interpretations and impressions.

(Please note I do not give grape varieties capital initials. I do not see how a grape variety constitutes a proper noun unless it forms part of the label, or the name, of the wine e.g. Cloudy Bay Sauvignon Blanc 1996.)

RED GRAPES

Variety	Most common descriptors	Spice	Regional variation
cabernet sauvignon	Blackcurrant, bell pepper (young wine)	Black pepper/mint/tobacco	Mostly textural, New World examples are more forward and softer.
cabernet franc	Strawberry, raspberry	Lead pencil/slate	New World jammier and riper.
pinot noir	Wild strawberry, cherry, truffles, well-hung game	n/a	New World juicier, looser and sweeter.
merlot	Prunes, plums, leather	White pepper	Warm climate: softer and sweeter. Cold climate: more rounded and savoury.
syrah	Blackberries, figs, blueberry, coffee	Cinnamon, pepper	New World spicier.
mourvèdre	Damsons, prunes	Black pepper	New World spicier.
grenache	Ripe plums	n/a	Old World richer. New World sweeter.
carignan	Underripe hedgerow fruit	n/a	New world sweeter.
cinsault	Plum jam	n/a	New World riper.
pinotage	Damsons, raspberry, blackberry, gamy, chocolate, rubber	All-spice	n/a.
zinfandel	Figs, raisins, blackcurrant, chocolate, leather	Black pepper, cinnamon	n/a
nebbiolo	Plums, raspberry, prunes, licorice	Anise	New World juicier. Italian most licorice.
sangiovese	Baked hedgerow fruit, earth	Black and white pepper	Old World earthier/tannic.
tannat	Old leather, soft fruit	Cardamom	n/a.
malbec	Wood, soft fruit, leafy	Pepper	New World juicier.
barbera	Licorice, plums, tea-leaf	Anise	Old World less tannic, more acidity.
dornfelder	Ripe plums, juicy	n/a	n/a.
gamay	Raspberry, cherry, apple, banana	n/a	Beaujolais higher in alcohol, sweeter, rounder.
tempranillo	Vanilla, plums, chocolate, tea, almonds	Paprika	Spanish the most chocolate.
kekfrancos	Ripe plums, leather, cherry	n/a	n/a

WHITE GRAPES

Variety	Most common descriptors	Spice	Regional variation
sauvignon blanc	Gooseberry, asparagus, cat's urine, grass	Nutty	New World richer. Old World can be smokier.
chardonnay	Melon, butter, lemon, honey, rotting hay, mango	n/a	Cool climate drier, more vegetal.
viognier	Peaches, apricots	Marzipan	New World sweeter.
semillon	Citrus, ripe satsuma	Lime zest	Difficult to define since so much used in blends, but New World is much riper.
chenin blanc	Wet wool (dry wine), waxy/honey (off-dry wine)	Talcum powder	New World much zingier and fresher.
tokay pinot-gris	Peaches, apricots, honey, cobnuts	Orange zest	n/a.
pinot gris	Nuts, underripe melon	n/a	Warm-climate examples are fatter.
gewürztraminer	Rose petals, lychees	Cinnamon	New World makes more rounded wines.
riesling	Apple, petroleum, paraffin, honey, lime	Fruit cake spiciness	Cold-climate examples have more mineral edge to the acidity, more advanced plasticine aromas, greater petroleum undertones when old.
pinot blanc	Underripe peach, nutty	Little	n/a.
scheurebe	Grapefruit	n/a	n/a.
viura/macabeo	Nutty picked early, floral picked normally	n/a	n/a.
trebbiano	Underripe melon, almonds - all somewhat neutral	n/a	n/a.
traminer	General floweriness	n/a	Richer in hotter climates and fuller textured.
verdicchio	Lemon, bitter almond, fresh	n/a	n/a.
verdelho	Dried apricots, peaches	musky	New World versions much richer and riper.
silvaner	Mountain stream	n/a	n/a.
marsanne	Melon, lemon cordial, butterscotch, toffee	Rare	New World examples have an added clotted quality.
melon	Freshness, nuttiness, rarely any eponymous qualities	n/a	As muscadet's maker, it is more neutral.
aligote	Pebble, stoniness and cleanness	n/a	Little, except a touch more richness in the New World.

My bin bag after a few weeks' tasting.

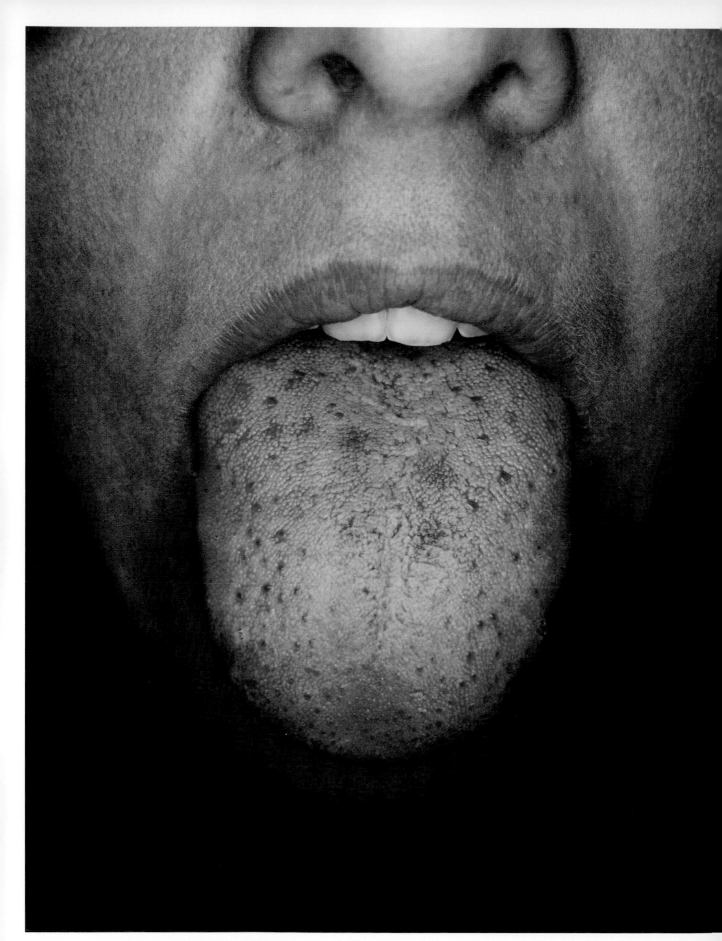

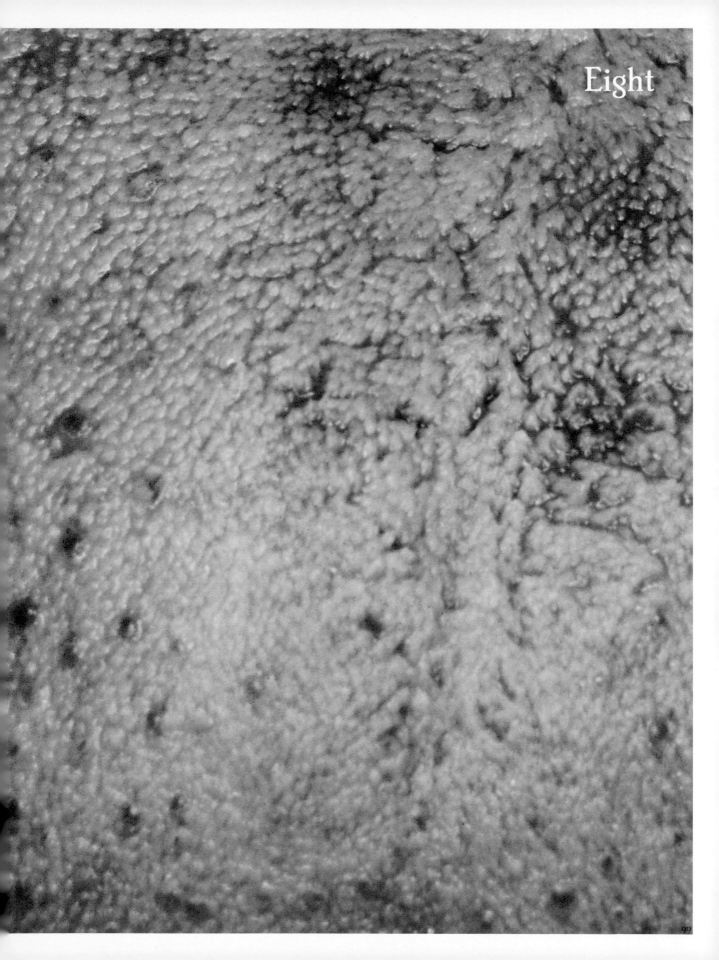

8 The Mysteries of Taste

(You've got it. It's only a matter of putting it to use)

The tongue: as individual as a fingerprint?

The tongue's sensitivity to sweetness is greatest at the tip, to bitterness at the base, to saltiness generally all round, and to sourness at the edges towards the centre. This is why it is important to swill wine around the mouth to stimulate all the taste receptors. But not everyone has the same number of these and, consequently, the ability to develop highly refined 'taste'. Research in America has shown that the differences in the number of taste-buds in people means that humankind can be divided into non-tasters, medium tasters, and super-tasters. How many people in the wine business, unbeknownst even to themselves, are medium or non-tasters possessing too few taste-buds for the job? This may explain why certain individuals professionally employed in wine cannot detect faults in wines. *Sommeliers*, to mention just one group, should be medically examined before getting their job. Discrimination is the ability to detect subtle differences in taste in this respect and if an individual lacks the tools for this, that is say, is born lacking the necessary number of taste-buds, then other avenues of employment are to be recommended. This is not to say, however, that such a person could not get a lot of enjoyment from wine.

Why does sugar need to be sweet? And acid sharp? Chemically, neither sensation is provable as one or the other in a laboratory. The sensations of sweetness and sharpness only exist when there is a palate to recognize them. Unless apprehended by the senses, neither sweetness nor acidity has value. By the same token, no machine can detect great wine from poor wine: structurally, the evidence for the difference hardly exists. *Great wine has no meaning, no existence, until we taste it and recognize it as such.*

Does this make wine drinkers Existentialists? Or merely Bacchants — our faith creating the creed? Whether we care for these labels or not, there is no escaping the fact that taste is a subjective, personal experience, important aspects of which only exist when we recognize their impact through taste. Thus, degrees of sweetness, dryness, fruitiness exist which only each individual can determine. What you may call very sweet I may characterize as merely fairly sweet. What you will term dry, I may consider subtly fruity or even honeyed.

Is it any wonder that the application of terms like dry, medium-dry, sweet or off-dry to wines means so very little in a general context? We can, as individuals, only truly understand what a wine producer means by any of these gradations when we taste the wine. Only then can we have a basis for judgement — agreement or disagreement.

What is a dry wine? No one knows. Many people who refuse to drink German wines, erroneously believing that their sweetness will not be to their taste, often love Australian chardonnay, for example. However, in actual fact not only may the German wine be technically drier — that is, contain less sugar — than the chardonnay from Australia, but even if it does contain more sugar its acidity will so balance the effect of the wine on the palate that rather than appear sweet it seems merely very fruity (again, just like the Aussie chardonnay).

Through a glass – darkly? dimly? dumbly? dangerously? dryly?

Perception plays a huge role in influencing our view of the sweetness or dryness of a wine. This is explored elsewhere in this book. In this chapter, which deals with the phenomenon of taste, it is first of all important to understand how infuriatingly imprecise an area we are examining here. Not only can we rarely describe a taste accurately to anyone else, we cannot even give it a name to ourselves. We truly do only recognize it when we taste it.

Taste is, then, unformulaic and nebulous. It is beyond our understanding to grasp what another person is experiencing when that person tastes a wine. It is the same when we listen to music. I do not mean by this simply that one person's meat is another person's poison. This liking for or loathing of some things above others goes without saying.

What, then, is taste? As a term it has crucial shades of meaning. It straddles the turbulent divide between personal preference and straightforward sensation. Even style enters into the picture with the modern twist given the word by fashionability. But our remit dictates we navigate only one tributary: taste is what you experience when wine comes into contact with your sensory system.

Smell is merely taste deferred

Once in the mouth, the presence of the wine sets all sorts of bells ringing in the brain. This in turn leads to an immediate increase in saliva production (inevitable but redundant since saliva helps soften food, hardly necessary with wine). These digestive juices contain their own enzymes which create chemical changes and help the body absorb the food in the right way. Whether one's saliva is as individual as one's DNA or thumbprint is open to argument, but certainly the individuality of saliva may contribute to each person's specific reaction to a wine.

As with smell, experience of tasting many wines over many years may permit you to arrive at a view of what variety of grape(s) a wine might have been made from, where those grapes were grown, certain processes the wine maker applied in the wine's manufacture, and an array of other debatable inferences from how well the wine will age over time to what kind of food it will best accompany.

Taste has the crucial role, above all else, of deciding whether we like the wine or not and if we do, how much we like it (a lot, not very much, a little, and possibly a dozen fine lines in between). Nothing to quarrel with here. Is it reasonable, in these circumstances, for the taster to attempt to go a step further and try to characterize the nature of that reaction in a way which involves references to taste? Of course. But the problem as I see it comes when taste is elevated to the position of primary validatory characteristic.

What I want to pin down here is the crucial centrality to wine tasting of the individuality of each nose, tongue, mouth and throat, nervous system, saliva flow, metabolism and outlook, in every single wine taster. We are free to determine the nature of the aroma and the taste of the wine in the glass in front of us in any way we care to choose.

Bacchants . . .

or Existentialists?

No rules which stand up to sensible scrutiny exist

To be sure, we cannot claim the wine is white if it is red. If we did, we would have an optical problem we would ourselves recognize as disabling in the context of wine differentiation and our opinion on colour, though entertaining, would be worthless. The same would apply if we claimed the wine was cloudy if it was crystal bright or if we reckoned the wine tasted like treacle when it contained no sugar above that naturally conferred by the sweetness of the alcohol. In these instances, the views our senses have caused us to form are freakish. They have value only to ourselves.

Wine is always a unique experience. None of us can ever know if someone else is experiencing the same sensation as we are when we both drink the same wine at the same time.

It is, then, more important for the taster to be confident in his or her own sense of what they personally and uniquely experience in a glass of wine, than to accept what I or any other so-called expert claims to find. There are no sacred rules to taste. We can only agree on, and this book can only offer, general ideas about how best to behave to achieve the optimum-tasting pleasure from a glass of wine and what constitutes manners in approaching that acquisition of pleasure.

You must find and be secure within your own realm of conscious wine appreciation. If you care too much about what someone else thinks or slavishly devote your critical faculties to absorbing another's line of reasoning, you will not develop a true individual appreciation of wine nor will you be able to contribute anything original to the tasting of it.

Don't tell me how it tastes. How does the wine feel?

Personally, I think texture is as vital as taste to the pleasure a wine can give yet, very few people will consider this is an aspect they should consciously comment on when asked for an immediate reaction to a glass of wine. Yet is not texture as important to a fruit as taste? What would an apple, for instance, taste like if it were not crisp? A pear soft? A coconut crunchy? A plum fleshy? Each fruit has a texture peculiar to it and we would not regard the fruit as up to standard if it did not display this texture characteristic. Soft apples are horrible. Hard pears are the same. Gooey pineapples are inedible.

Notwithstanding these crucial elements of how a fruit delivers its individual flavour, the wine taster is always invited, even expected, to think in terms of taste alone — apart from, I suppose, clichés like velvety as applied to certain rich reds. Yet it is texture which helps determine how well the wine will go with food. What use the much-vaunted complex flavours of a wine when it comes up against any dish? Those flavours will, largely, be lost or diminished.

Drinkers are expected to think in the terms which they have been schooled (or bullied) into believing are the proper ones; it is only in these terms that they can describe the wine and characterize it to themselves or any enquirer. Thus taste rules the mental roost. Wine buyers, merchants and critics all follow this path. It can hardly be wrong. (I'm not concerned with wrongness or rightness here in any case.) It simply isn't very helpful, honest, realistic or of any value. For if, as I contend, taste is so personal an experience as to be unknowable to anyone else in the same way, what good does it do anyone else to be told what our taste has found?

Goodnessness and graciousness

What good it does to be told what a wine tastes of? It serves to characterize how an individual has found the wine. I do not myself, in reviewing a wine, eschew writing that I have, for example, found the taste of marmalade (in a moscatel de Valencia), overripe melon (in certain Australian chardonnays), cricket bats (in retsina), cassis (in a cabernet sauvignon) or leather (in a merlot), but in all these instances the fruit analogies listed are almost substitutes for the grape variety, wine style and provenance. That is to say that a retsina which doesn't taste of cricket bats (a fanciful way of characterizing the resinated, turpentine flavour of the wine) isn't a retsina at all — or certainly it is so untypical of the type as to be misnamed. All right, this is an extreme example, but the rest are not so extreme and I could quote many others (gooseberries and sauvignon blanc, say).

What purpose, then, is being served in employing a taste factor if it does no more than restate the obvious? It satisfies the human urge to classify things, to pigeon-hole them, to parcel them up and put them where they belong. Isn't that what discrimination is about? It permits the exercise of the critical faculties in a way which demonstrates Holmesian prowess — that is to say the ability to deduce from recognized evidence certain inalienable, common-sense facts. Curiously, it seems to me that this approach is the very opposite of common-sensical if all it does is to provide a focus which blurs the edges of wine rather than providing, as it is intended to do and assumed to achieve, a clear exposé of a wine's charms and an erudite analysis of why it is the way it is. Texture is as important to a wine as the script is to a movie. In both cases, star billing is credited elsewhere — and who ever remembers the name of the scriptwriter anyway?

Paul Vogel. Born 6:5:66 @ 12.35pm

Nine

Julian Vogel. Born 6:5:66 @ 12.40pm

9 The All-Star Cast

(Or how to get out of wine what's gone into it)

Every single glass you pour from the same bottle is a different wine. Heraclitus pointed out 2500 years ago that you cannot step twice into the same river and so it is that you cannot drink of precisely the same wine from the same bottle twice. The wine, like the river, may have the same name and source but just as the river's flow creates a constantly changing liquidity so it is with wine. To be sure, you only dramatically appreciate the difference over an extended period of time, an hour or two, maybe, or if left for days or weeks (when you would immediately sense the onset of vinegariness), but a wine will undergo subtle changes from minute to minute as air develops its bouquet and fruit. You would also, perhaps, detect minor differences in the taste of the wine from fresh bottles of the same vintage drunk several months apart. What this demonstrates is that wine is not only sensitive to exposure to air but is also a maturing artefact individual to each bottling.

The effect of air on an opened bottle of wine is the beginning of the death of that wine. It has only a comparatively short time to live, to be agreeable to our senses, before it becomes unpleasant to a greater or lesser degree. We can smell and taste the decline of or the improvement in a very old wine, once it has been in the glass and air been permitted to get to all of it, as from the moment of the bottle's opening and within ten minutes. Air is both friend and enemy. Time is what decides which it will be. Infinity, like immortality, is not, however, an option.

This is the area of a wine's performance over which its makers have little control. The wine is out of their hands. They may provide advice as to how long they consider the wine may be cellared in an assumed optimum state prior to its drinking and they may offer a view as to how long the wine may be left to breathe, having been decanted, prior to being served. More than this they cannot do.

Between the first planting of the vines which gave of their grapes to make the wine and the pouring of that wine into the drinker's glass — its moment of birth as a consumable liquid — the factors which affect the taste of wine are threefold. All of which involve human intervention.

One: First, there is the inherent taste of the fruit offered by the particular grape variety (or clone of the variety) as it is grown in its unique vineyard situation and greater regional siting.

Two: Then there are the viticultural factors, that is to say those which occur naturally or are caused to happen in the vineyard as the vines go through a growing season.

Three: Finally, there are oenological factors, which are those made manifest by the wine maker's approach to the grapes at harvest picking, his or her level of interference and techniques of intervention during wine making, and the manner of the ageing of the wine and then its blending — either with barrels or tanks of the same grape or with several other grape varieties.

Thus we can assemble an impressive cast of actors starring in a wine, among which are those that account for the reason, as any seasoned burgundy drinker, for example, will testify, why two bottles of wine from the same designated vineyard in the same appellated area from exactly the same clone of the same grape picked at precisely the same time can taste decidedly different. (It is outside the scope of this book to examine why this utterly undermines the credibility of the French wine laws which are based on the notion of the supposedly eternal excellence of a given plot of ground. The vagaries — within the rules — of the individual growing grapes on it do nothing to deny this plot its status.) Of all the (f)actors which comprise the cast of *The Taste of Wine*, none receives bigger billing than the grape.

The grape — the raisin d'être of all wine

A grape as a gathered fruit, and we are not concerned with any one particular variety here, has component parts each of which affects the taste of the finished wine. These are the skin, the pulp, the pips, and the stalks. To a large extent, the latter may be discarded; only a few wine makers use stalks any more, almost exclusively in red wines for tannin extraction, and it requires some degree of experience and traditional usage to utilize sympathetically the bitter tannins which come from stalks.

The Rhône, for example, has several stalk fans. Some growers ('wine maker' is not a term used in traditional areas like the Rhône), with the most expensive wines of this region, prefer the finer style that a totally destalked crop offers; others never destalk and get longer-lived but arguably coarser wines (certainly in their youth). Certain growers will probably remove stalks if the grapes are not as ripe as normal. The reason for this is to achieve a better balance in the finished wine; with less natural sugar in the grapes, too much tannin from the stalks might overpower the fruit and though it would result in a wine which needed to be cellared in order to soften the tannin, this maturing would see a decline in the fruit.

The fruit and tannin balance in a red wine which is designed to age, a so-called *vin de garde*, is crucial. One small appellated Rhône village which still traditionally uses stalks for all its red wines — certainly in this drinker's experience — is Rasteau in the southern Rhône; other pockets of stalkdom in France and in Europe exist. For most other wine makers, the stage prior to pressing or crushing the grapes will involve stem removal and discarding, perhaps mechanically by an auger. The pips are carried on into the wine-making process — this is unavoidable — but only with red wine is there any great chance of them being crushed and the tannins they contain being released.

The skin — more than a mere protective coat

A wine's colour is derived from the grapes' skin. That is why red wine is red. White wine made from darker-coloured grapes can only be white because the amount of time the skins have spent in contact with the juice is limited. The wine maker exercises judgement and keeps an eye on the clock. Skin contact, called by the French *macération pelliculaire*, varies in its length of time; with white grapes making white wine it can be much longer than with red grapes for white wine, since with the former only a straw or golden hue will result even if the contact time is several days. White grapes do not possess the anthocyanic chemicals, the colouring matter, of red grapes.

The chemicals from the grape skin affect the taste. These so-called flavour compounds occur in the skin, and of course in the flesh which makes up the bulk of the juice, and they have been the subject of increasing debate and scientific scrutiny over the past twenty years. Several have been discovered and identified and applied to specific grape varieties. In the usual fashion, elongated polysyllabic Greco-Roman vehicles, the stretch-limos of all scientific disciplines, have been constructed to carry these compounds' names. This is a specialized area and only the scientifically-oriented taster needs bother with it.

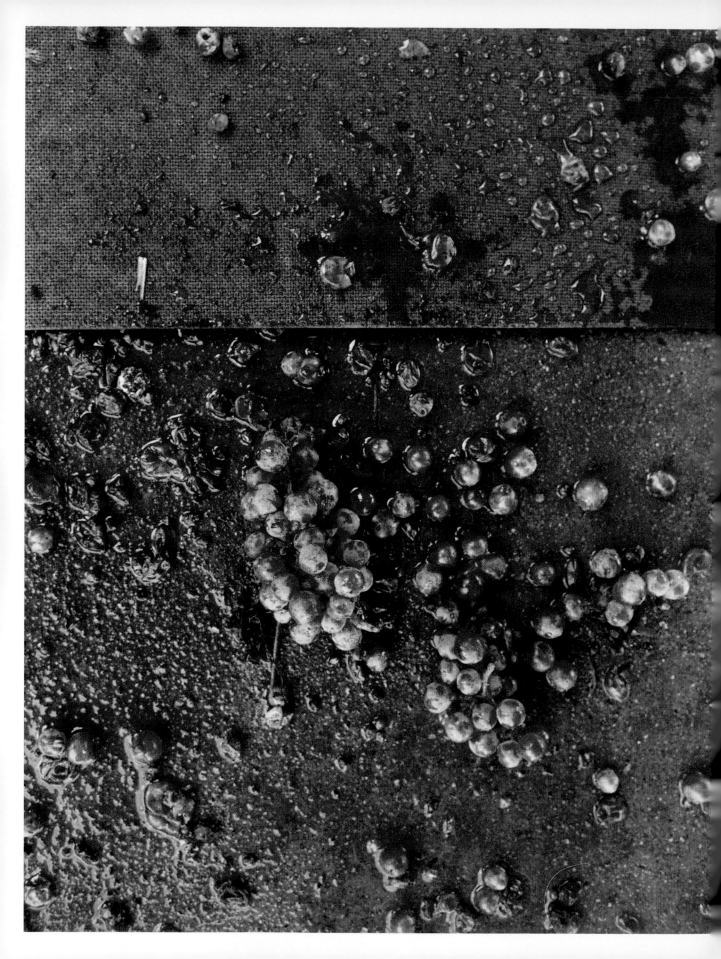

The skin of the grape also contributes potassium, given the deliciously Kafkaesque chemical letter K (for Kalium), and though this is monumentally important to the balance of a wine's structure and balance because of its dramatic role in acid levels, it is not important to the taster. As far as I know, no taster is yet able, nor would ever be able, I suggest, to discern from a sensory assessment of wine's acidity status what the concentration of potassium might have been in the grape skins. Who would wish even to consider concentrating his mind upon this? Not the ordinary taster in the street certainly. The chemist in the wine laboratory and the wine maker might be keen to know and they have the equipment and the methods to measure it. Of greater import to the taster is tannin.

Tannin — you can't beat it

A notable contributor to the structure of a wine, red wine particularly but also certain whites undergoing extended skin-contact time, is tannin. Tannin, I often think, is like a building's inner brickwork. It holds the wine up in many instances yet is not obvious to certain senses: eye or nose. It has little colour to contribute (though it is similar in chemical structure to wine's colouring agents) and being without aroma it cannot be detected on the nose — though having said that I almost never find a rich deep wine with a compelling aroma which does not possess tannin in some degree or other and, just like the brickwork invisible behind the elegant plaster moulding of a fine building, contributes something which if it were absent would not permit the complexity of the surface to be so bold. This has no basis in scientific fact, you understand. It is merely thirty-odd years of empirical boozing offering a point of view.

With white wine, the presence of tannin is less often sensed — by me at least — although without doubt the lifted aroma of a deep golden chardonnay, for example, which has been produced with a certain amount of skin-contact time will have some tannin. It is possible to measure tannin. A so-called gallic acid test will reveal that the average white wine has something less than one-sixth of the tannin in an average red.

The etymology of the word gallic itself tells us something about the nature of tannin. Gall is the name given to the intense bitter substance which is a secretion of the liver and also to that bitter condition of the human spirit which in olden times was believed to have been linked to the gall bladder — i.e. resentment or rancour. We say of an experience which is irritating that it is galling. Gall is also an excrescence found on trees, oaks especially, which have been infested or visited by gall-flies, cynips so-called, which pierce the bark and lay eggs which become oak-galls or gall-apples; instead of bringing forth baby cynips these are gathered, or used to be, to manufacture ink, tannin for curing animal skins, and even in some instances for use in certain medicines.

Tannin doesn't, then, sound at all pleasant to have around, let alone find in a glass of wine. It is, however, a massive contributor to the texture and personality of red wine. It is the harmony between tannin and a wine's fruit, acid and, very importantly, alcohol which creates the conditions both for longevity, the potential to develop more impressively in feel and flavour over some years, and for the more immediate and engaging texture — plus an all-important food compatibility — of a younger wine designed to be drunk within a couple of years.

Tannin also contributes to red wine's widely recognized benefits as a 'health' drink, when taken in moderation This is because the phenolic compounds in a wine of which tannin is a part inhibit the oxidative characteristics of low-density lipoproteins, a factor in the development of atherosclerosis. As an antioxidant tannin therefore contributes to the lessening of the conditions in the body which can lead to coronary heart disease. It is hardly within the scope of this book to examine all this in great scientific depth, but isn't it comforting to know that wine drinking has a basis not just in civilized conviviality but in a lifestyle which is genuinely better for you?

Tannin is instantly detectable by the shrivelling up of the sides of the mouth and the back and back-sides of the tongue. In an aggressively tannic young wine the flesh of the mouth cavity is sensing the process by which an animal skin is transformed when tannin is used to tan hides; it reacts with the collagen in the animal skin to produce what English-speaking humankind is pleased to call leather.

Tannin — a short historical digression

Like the serendipitous collusion of freshly picked grapes and fire in a damp cave many thousands of years ago which first kindled in human beings the idea of the metamorphosis of fruit juice into alcohol, a process we now call fermentation, it is likely that the turning into leather of animal skins, which rotted when wet and became unbearably stiff when dry, was first developed when early hunters noted that their clothes were better preserved when water off the barks of trees dripped on them. The ancient Egyptians were skilled tanners but it wasn't until around 1880 that the chemical science of the process was understood. Tanners would get their tannin from a variety of exotic sources that read like a magical elixir: the acorns of the Levantine oak, mimosa bark, quebracho wood from Mexico and other parts of South America, certain cuttings from Borneo, the Indian myrabolam nut, and sumac leaves and leaves from the Far Eastern uncaria gambir plant. No doubt the Worshipful Company of Tanners possessed just as many refined sensibilities as the Worshipful Company of Wine Snobs and boasted members who with one sniff of a shoe upper or the front seat of a new Singer Le Mans Tourer could tell you whether the tanning agent derived from a Turkish acorn or a Malay rubber plant.

Tannin can claim for itself a lengthy history crammed with incident. For the wine taster, an understanding of it is crucial. As the minor historical digression in the box demonstrates, tannin softens and preserves; its presence affects a wine's shape and performance, over and above its impact on the senses in several ways:

One: Tannin permits red wine to age. The oldest red wine I ever purchased, a Pauillac of the 1934 vintage, was over fifty years of age when drunk and it was in perfect condition, went deliciously with an old barnyard fowl roasted with forty cloves of garlic, and its tannin would have permitted it to age agreeably for another dozen years. The balance of elements of the wine was remarkable and very fine. I have no doubt that the wine would have tasted aggressive and spiky if it had been drunk within a couple of years of release. The tannins needed chastening over time. My fifty-year-old Pauillac was carefully decanted because of the sedimented tannins. It began to decline in vigour in the glass only as the last drop disappeared, some three hours after opening.

Two: Tannin is only one element in a wine. Fruit sugar, acidity, alcohol also play their parts and these are all present in a fine wine in such disposition that none will robustly intimidate the others. If there is disequilibrium the wine cannot mature to balanced fineness. Such a wine may be interesting and very drinkable but if it lacks poise, balance and readiness for the human palate when it is at its peak of maturity, it can never be termed a great wine deserving of huge reputation.

As alike as day-old chicks? Hmm . . .

200 years of tannin deposit in a venerable madeira.

Three: Tannin can be tamed by the intervention of food. This occurs in the same way that high acidity in a white wine can become ameliorated and softened when it is matched with appropriate food. Tannin in a young wine may have prospects to age well over five or six years, say, and allows the liquid to snare the flavours of a dish rather as the barbs in a hook ensure the fish is held firmly. The traditional British pairing of rare roast beef and claret is not simply sentimental but based on a fusion of chemical elements which genuinely do get on splendidly together: tannin and blood.

Four: For the taster, the presence of tannin and the hazarding of a guess as to its likely staying power over years is one of the trickiest decisions to reach. It might seem easy to come to the conclusion that a wine with loads of tannin will age for years. But the sugar and acidity must keep pace with the tannin and not give out before the tannin has softened and amalgamated better with these other aspects of a wine. I am often forced to conclude that a heavily tannic bordeaux will require so many years of ageing to knock the tannins into pleasant shape that by the time this blissful state is reached the fruit will be knackered or the acidity gone.

Five: Tannin must be balanced with alcohol. This is one of the areas of wine making requiring assured mastery. It is possibly the most scientifically difficult to bring under a measure of appreciation and control. Certain highly alcoholic Californian zinfandels, 14.5 per cent or so, which take several years to age to ripe lushness (though I must confess I personally really like them younger with rich food), are remarkably well balanced in spite of this weight of alcohol because of the richly muscled tannins present. An exceptional Châteauneuf-du-Pape of 13.5 per cent alcohol, which seems routine for this appellation, will only be fine if it has tannins to balance this force. Many examples nowadays strike me as lacking in the tannins to support such a percentage of alcohol.

Six: How can the taster estimate the worth of tannin in wine? There is only one answer to this question. You have to drink a lot and make written notes: your memory, however much you may trust it, is not entirely to be relied upon. Experience is the only teacher, once you have learned to recognize tannin and identify the balance of its relationship with the other elements. How do you learn to ride a bicycle or master the art of walking a tightrope? Surely it begins with a single step...

Seven: Wood tannins. Up until now the type of tannin under discussion has been fruit tannin, that is to say, tannin derived directly from the grapes. But tannin is also found in wood. In new wood, oak used in wine barrels, tannin passes into the wine from the staves, the convex planks forming the barrel's rotundity, and the butt ends, the circles of wood at either end, and this may be of a distinctive type which some tasters can identify. (Wood and its influences upon the smell and taste of wine are discussed in Chapter 12.)

To sum up: tannin is a tricky customer for the taster to evaluate

What is a tannic wine? Tannin shares, along with loose descriptions such as 'sweet' or 'demi-sec' (about which the views of no two tasters rarely coincide), the distinction of being very much a matter of individual preference which may range from hostility through to uncritical devotion, with in the middle the knowledge-seeking stance of the drinker who merely wants to know how a particular wine will age and for how long. It is not even possible to create a table aiming at some kind of correlation between weight of tannin and the likely life of wines. The taster judges the balance of tannin along with the fruit, acid, and alcohol on the palate, and arrives at a judgement taking all these aspects into account.

The flesh — the juice provider

There are certain varieties of grapes the flesh of which is red or reddish-pink. Called by the French *teinturiers* or dyer varieties, they were active in the bad old days when there was a lack of colour from the major varieties. They were used purely to provide a more acceptably vivid hue. Their existence need detain us no further.

The great majority of wine grapes, whatever the colour of their skins, have pale flesh. If no skins are used in making a wine the flesh yields a primary juice which is a sort of neutral grey, sometimes chalky, at times somewhat medicinal in aspect, and rarely ever, in my experience at least, especially appetizing to behold.

Flesh contributes the bulk of the grape juice and certain major elements of the finished wine. It is useful to recognize here just how important to the character of the finished wine are the sugars, acids and minerals which the grape berry has absorbed and acted upon during its fruition period. These sugars, acids and minerals are shaped and deeply affected by the circumstances of their upbringing:

One: The climate.
Two: The vine's location and soil.
Three: The grower's treatment of the vines.

For the highly specialized taster, especially one deeply versed in the wines of a particular vineyard region, the appearance, aroma and taste of a wine from that region provide precise clues to all these things.

The grape flesh, since its outermost part contains pathways which have carried the water and minerals emanating from the vine roots as well as the sugar made via the photosynthesis of the leaves, is in this way influenced differently every vintage year, which is why there are such differences between wines of different years from the same vineyard. Each year the grape juice is different; different in style, content, make-up, and potential to make interesting wine. Each year, also, the wine maker is a different person; not merely because of the accretions to skill which maturity brings but because of differences in temperament and personality which age may develop. Even a wine maker in late middle age may have been involved in as few as thirty vintages. Craftspersons and scientists in disciplines other than oenology do what they do on a daily or weekly basis and become quickly acclimatized, but the wine maker has an apprenticeship which lasts a lifetime.

This is not widely appreciated by drinkers and in many ways it accounts for why wine making is such a trying business. Trial and error is often the only way to discover new ideas and though modern wine makers are prodigious readers of the technical wine press world-wide, the learning curve of necessity stretches far. No wine maker can claim to have seen everything when he only gets to handle fruit once a year and never the same fruit twice. (The so-called flying wine makers who vinify various wines in different parts of the world each year are exposed to a greater width of experiences but not necessarily depth. Their work-style does not give them the insight into wine from or the growing conditions within a single vineyard which is the wealth of experience accruing to the *vigneron* devoted to his lone patch.)

The Vintex Report

Each year in a vineyard is always a unique occurrence. A single regional year has been most fascinatingly documented by Vintex, the Bordeaux wine dealers. This report, detailed as it is, admittedly provides a general picture, and certainly individual vineyards will have their own variances within this generality; nevertheless the document that follows not only confirms that each year is a fresh struggle but that the victory at the end of it, that year's wine, is always sensorily different and, in many ways, a different wine from different berries and different vines (one year older and wiser). Family resemblances between vintages will always exist, however.

I am grateful to Vintex, especially to Mr William Blatch, the company's president and the report's author, for permission to reprint in full the report they sent me in November 1997. I have asterisked certain technical terms and these are explained at the end of the report.

VINTEX S.A.

370, Boulevard Alfred Daney W
33300 BORDEAUX – FRANCE

Preliminary Bordeaux Vintage Report

1997 has proved to be the most difficult recent vintage to assess. It has been a vintage of such irregularity, both in the ripening cycle of the grapes, and in the weather's effect on them, that it is almost impossible to generalize about its overall character. As soon as one vat tastes 'typical' for the vintage, the next one is completely different: some lighter, some heavier, some more acid, some totally soft.

It has been a year when the vine acted slowly, even sometimes completely shut down, so it was often a laborious year, with the vine arriving at each successive stage of its cycle with considerable difficulty. However, fortunately, the day chosen for the harvest to begin was the earliest in any year since 1899, making the earliest vintage of the century, so there were always a few spare weeks in the pocket for catching up.

In the end, those who created situations where their vines could arrive at total ripeness have made some excellent wines, in some cases superior to their '96s; the rest anything from just acceptable to very good. Growers found it such a toil that few seemed to have the energy afterwards to show the enthusiasm a lot of these wines deserve.

Now back to the beginning of the story.

A warm winter

The winter only really lasted from 26 December to 15 January. During this period, the sap went right down into the roots, especially during the period of permanent frost 26 December–4 January. It was just this tiny period that ensured that the vines relaxed and that the last year's generation of pests could be killed off.

Without this cold snap, the winter would have been a record for warmth. Outside of it, it only froze on four other nights. Before it, the mean December temperature was 1.5°C over the average, and after it, the mean temperatures grew progressively: 2.3°C over the average in January, 3.3°C over in February, 3.4°C over in March.

This meant that the vine was raring to go at any moment, especially as soil moisture was generally satisfactory. There was sufficient water-retention from the summer rainfall of 1996, and November had been very wet. So the water tables were only 20 per cent from full at the end of the two comparatively dry months of December and January, during which rainfall was only 50 per cent of average. When 65 mm of rain fell during the first three weeks of February (normal), and with maximum temperatures climbing to a full 5.3°C over the average in the last week, swellings began to be seen everywhere.

Budding

The vines took longer to bud than in 1996. This was the origin of the irregular bunch-to-bunch ripening cycle. Many merlots and sauvignons got to the 'pointe verte' stage,* at least on the two or three lower buds, during the first week of March. The full bud-burst stage, however, got spun out, generally happening over the 8−9 March weekend on the warmer, more gravelly soils, and up to the 18th on the cooler soils.

In general, budding was assessed to be two weeks ahead of schedule, with the exception of parts of the Médoc which had received less rainfall and which consequently had less sap up with which to do it. If this advance could be maintained up to flowering, that would mean a very early vintage, the so-called 'vin de mars',* which usually means quality too. On the other hand, it brought with it the virtual certainty of post-budding frost. The 'Lune Rousse',* traditional harbinger of spring frost, was due to fall on 21−22 April, the anniversary of the terrible 1991 frost. With demand for bordeaux already very strong, the négoce* started taking precautions, and transactions for bulk bordeaux rouge hit an all-time record in both February and March.

April

With March afternoon temperatures soaring to 6.6°C over the average maximum, the shoots grew fast and vigorously. But, as the month wore on, and got drier and drier (only 15 mm fell during the whole month: 80 per cent less than the average), the foliage growth slowed, and, by early April, the leaves were beginning to curl and the whole vineyard took on a strange pale olive-grove colour.

The first eleven days of April saw even hotter afternoons: always over 20°C, once (the 11th) at 25°C, as an unusual sirocco wind blew air into Bordeaux from the Mauritanian Sahara, yet the night-time temperatures were often close to 0°C. Such variations of temperature on such far-advanced foliage further stressed the vines, and the leaves curled up even more. But the real worry was about frost. The 'Lune Rousse' was approaching, but, even if we got through that unharmed, it is the 'Saints de Glace',* still a month away (11−12−13 May) that are always supposed to be the true end of the frost risk.

On 18 April, the lead story of the 1 o'clock news was about the previous night's frost in the Côtes du Ventoux.* Médoc growers that day were not at ease, but happy to be working in 20°C conditions. The Arctic air that had been sucked into Eastern France around a Low over Russia had not yet stopped the Westerlies coming in over Bordeaux. But, when another little Low formed over NW Spain and then moved into the Mediterranean, part of that Arctic air was diverted over Western France too, arriving in Bordeaux on the morning of the 22nd just after daybreak. At 5 a.m., it was 9° in Bordeaux − by 8 a.m., it was down to 4°, just in time to be countered by the heat from sunlight. It had been a close call: if that mass of air had arrived three hours earlier in the pre-dawn chill, a lot of wine would have been lost. In the end, apart from a few vineyards in Barsac, Graves and Eastern Entre-Deux-Mers, most properties only lost a few bunches here and there, but, when these subsequently counterbudded two weeks later, it only added to the irregularity problem that was to come at the flowering.

But the 'Lune Rousse' had been faithful to its reputation, and the following nights, nobody was going to take any chances: The whole of that area of Barsac, etc. was swathed in a veil of black smoke from the rubber tyres that were set alight − in spite of the ecologists' protests (which were quickly countered by a statement from the President of the Sauternes Union that the growers were 'des citoyens responsables qui savent prendre en main leur avenir').*

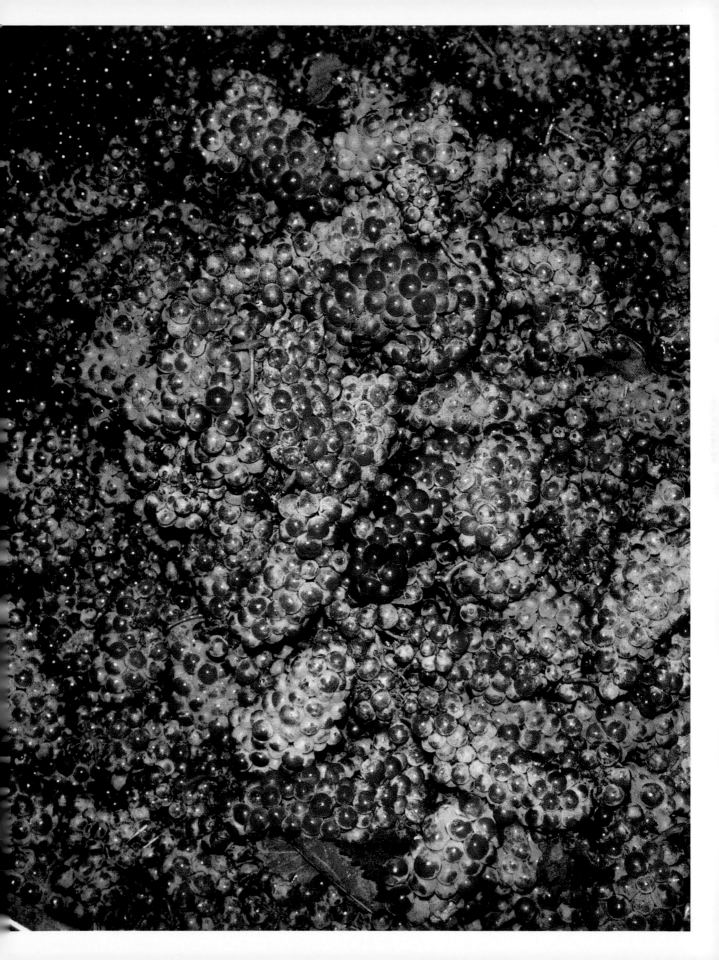

There was one more night of damage two days later on the 24th, this time confined mostly to Pessac-Leognan and SE Médoc, which will account for shortages in the Leognan crus classes and in some Margaux, Listrac and Moulis wines, but quickly thereafter, the South wind returned, bringing temperatures up to an amazing 29°C on 2 May.

Flowering

In the last week of April, the soil was parched from lack of rain (1—25 April: 0 mm), and the vine was gasping. Yet it wanted to flower. The first stamens were seen over the weekend of 3—4 May on warm-soil merlots and sauvignons. These had been brought on by the 30 April—5 May heat-wave, but the process was accelerated by the showers that fell 26—28 April and 5—6 May, producing just enough water to invigorate the vine once more.

It was at this point that one of the vintage's most important features was determined: the flowering now got spun out by the cold nights of 7—8 May, by the rain-squalls of 10—19 May, and by the sudden cold nights of 20—22 (the week of the London Wine Trade Fair). To make matters worse, a loose high pressure system stagnated over E. Europe 25—31 May, bringing a sudden blast of 30°C temperatures into the region, just at the end of the flower, as the 'nouaison'* was in process.

Such variable conditions during flowering are not good, and resulted in coulure* and millerandage* just about everywhere, but especially on the warmer-soil merlots (Pomerol — as in '96, St-Emilion, in particular) and on the sauvignons. Once again, as in 1996, this will mean reduced yields in the top Pomerols and some St-Emilions (often the same areas as those hit by the April frosts).

More importantly for the whole of Bordeaux, these variable conditions created an acutely irregular start to the ripening cycle. Very generally, this concerned the merlots more than the cabernets, the sauvignons more than the semillons, and, as luck would have it, these were the very two varieties that were to suffer the most from the end-of-August rain: a double reason for the greater potential of semillon and cabernet in 1997.

By 30 May, all of the flowering was completed, but it had taken a full month to do so. (cf 1996: twelve days approx). We have had irregular flowerings before, but the irregularity had always been from vineyard to vineyard, vine to vine, occasionally bunch to bunch. This time, the irregularity was inside the bunch: in one bunch, individual grapes flowered at different times. Clearly this was going to be a difficult vintage to pick. With Hale-Bopp now over the horizon, the Year of the Comet was maybe not going to be so easy as we had imagined.

But maybe the extreme earliness of the flowering could still ensure a grand millésime? After all, a fantastic summer could iron out a lot of the irregularity, as it often has done in the past, and maybe the extraordinarily hot spring weather could be followed by fabulous summer weather. 1997 would then be not only the Year of the Comet, but also the Year of El Nino, and the enormous price increases that were now being asked for En Primeur 1996 Crus Classés could be repeated in 1997?

The Institut put the mid-flowering date at 23 May, which is twenty-two days ahead of the average, and the earliest since records have been kept. The previous earliest date was 27 May for the 1952 and 1990 vintages. In spite of the spring drought, the two-week advance at budding had become a three-week advance after flowering.

The Summer

For the three weeks following the flowering, the dream looked as though it could indeed come true after all: the end of May was a heat-wave, and the first two weeks of June, although humid, were permanently in the high 20s°C, even twice over 30°C; rainfall was moderate, and that of May had been sufficient to relieve the drought. But somehow the vine just didn't seem to want to play. The very long bunches of quite large grapes just didn't seem to evolve. All sorts of reasons were given at the time: the vine's stress from lack of water in April, the stretched-out flowering, the lack of rest from the warm winter. These all had something to do with it, but above all, the vine reacted very negatively to the cold snap at the end of the flowering. This had sent it dormant again, even altered its hormonal constitution, so that thereafter it never gave the bunches the required nourishment.

Then the weather broke: the Vinexpo* week was cool, with occasional showers. After that, the last ten days of June were seriously wet and cold: 107 mm of rainfall (654 per cent more than the average), and an average temperature 2.9°C lower than the average. It didn't clear up until 5 July.

This period was beset with potential dangers. First of all, oidium* had never been far away during the formation of the leaves and needed to be treated again. Mildew* was never much of a problem, but the grapes themselves were becoming prone to grey rot.* They had developed in size with the June rain and some of them had split and begun to rot. In addition, the other big feature of 1997, 'pourriture acide',* was beginning to spread around the split grapes, where the juice had attracted insects, which then further infected the bunches, giving them a nasty volatile smell* and orange appearance. This happened especially on the white grapes, above all on the sauvignons. All these problems obliged all conscientious growers to modify spraying programmes, to snip out any deteriorating grapes, and to crop-thin the bigger clusters ('vendange verte').*

Thereafter, rainfall was low for the rest of July, but the usual heat that we normally associate with this month never came. On the contrary, the month was cool and humid. Only three days saw temperatures rise over 30°C, making a total to date of seven days, which compares to an average of ten days, and to twenty-three days in the very dry year of 1995.

Such conditions encouraged the vine to grow very fast, but did not help the development of the grapes. The foliage had to be top-trimmed more frequently than usual. In addition, a lot of growers started 'effeuillage': leaf-elimination at the bottom around the bunches, to provide air-circulation.

Véraison*

The mid-véraison was reported by the Institut at 31 July, which meant that the vine had none the less maintained the earliness it had had at flowering. The two previous records for early flowering, 1952 and 1990, had been at mid-véraison at 3 and 6 August respectively. However, at this point, 1997 grapes, swollen by the June rains, were 40 per cent bigger than those of 1990 and 30 per cent bigger than the average.

Yet their sugar readings were actually higher and acidities about the same as 1990. At this point, if the grapes could 'lose weight' from a burst of dry hot weather, there was still a chance of a great vintage. After all, in 1982 and 1989, similar early-season moisture had caused the same difficulties in controlling disease, and 1990 had experienced something of the same irregularity.

Optimistic that this irregularity could be the only big remaining problem, many properties, having already done a 'vendange verte', now embarked on a 'vendange rose',* picking out all the bunches that were late in their véraison. Now, all that would be needed for this great vintage to come about was perfect weather up to the harvest.

August

At first this is exactly what happened: on 25 July, the weather had changed, and the traditional high pressure summer system developed over the region for a full month. This year, it was perfectly centred over France — normally its centre is over the Atlantic — with the result that the winds had more south in them, producing higher temperatures, and more effectively driving off any low-pressure systems that may come in over the Atlantic. During this period 25 July to 25 August, it was permanently 3.5°C hotter than the average, with fourteen days at 30°C+. This is the same as the scorching year of 1995 and only one day below 1990 which has the record.

However, unlike the baking heat of 1990 and 1995 that dried the grapes into little peas, August 1997 was not only hot: it was damp too. Not that it rained a lot, apart from the 37 mm that fell 4–10 August, it was just very humid, largely occasioned by the moist nature of these Southerlies as they came over the Pyrenees. The result was that, in such tropical conditions, the vine acted like a tropical plant, favouring its foliage, to which it gave all its energy. Consequently, in spite of all the efforts of the vigneron to trim the upper leaves, cut the lower leaves off, and crop-thin the retarded and spoilt bunches, all this heat never really produced the expected concentration.

18 August: The white harvest starts

Amidst a fanfare of publicity, the white harvest commenced in half a dozen Pessac-Leognan properties on Monday, 18 August. A syndicated news release quoted 1997 as 'already a legendary vintage: There is no doubt this will be exceptional'. Indeed, this was the earliest start of any vintage since 1893. The reputation of the vintage was further bolstered by first analyses of the musts at over 13° and total acidities of less than 5 g.*

However, it soon became clear that only a tiny part of the sauvignon harvest in this small corner of Bordeaux was showing so well. Elsewhere, we were not yet at ripeness and the grapes were looking fragile to say the least. In addition, the pickers whose smiling faces adorned the newspapers on the 19th were only keeping a small proportion of the grapes, leaving the greener berries to ripen further, and dropping to the ground the rotten or 'aigre' bunches.*

Other white properties, especially the lesser ones who had been less careful during the summer, started picking on Monday, 25 August. This received much less publicity. The grapes were rotting before they got to ripeness and had to be harvested in haste, often by machine, even the later-maturing semillons as well as the earlier, riper sauvignons. A lot of this part of the white harvest was not at all good.

The main part of the whites, however, were due to be picked from 1st September. Unfortunately, on 25 August, our high-pressure system that had been with us for a full month, weakened and moved south, allowing a succession of Atlantic fronts to move in over the region. On 25, 28 and 29 August, it rained heavily, and there were violent storms on the evening of the 27th.

When the sun came out again for the weekend of 30—31 August, there was a feeling of relief, but there were clearly certain vineyards that had suffered. Most remaining white properties started on Monday, 1 September. But the conditions that day were thunders. Many areas caught an unwanted 35—40 mm rainfall in that single day; others were relatively spared. So some had to delay to the Tuesday whilst others could start.

During the first few days of this week, the vendange contained a bit of everything: some musts had very low sugar levels; others had a good 11°—11.5°. Some very sick-looking emergency-picked semillons came in alongside some very aromatic healthy sauvignons. Some of the muscadelles, always the most fragile grape, had to be simply thrown away. A lot depended on the vineyard work carried out through the summer.

By the weekend of 6—7 September, the sun had been out for five days, and although the mornings were misty, the days were hot and dry, and those healthier sections of the whites that could wait produced some very solid, full-styled semillons right up to the 11th. These musts were rich and full, and reminded everyone of the big fat '90s.

Many of the more prestigious properties continued picking even later, harvesting, in successive 'tries'* à la sauternes, only those bunches that became successively ripe. Some of those Pessac-Leognan châteaux that had started 18—19 August picked their last whites on 26 September, their longest harvest on record. These pickers had been in the vineyard almost constantly since early July, manually snipping, sorting, thinning, and now they had to spend five weeks at the harvest doing the same thing again. They got to know each vine pretty well, and a year like this has taught everyone a lot about their vineyard. We will certainly be seeing the benefits of this experience in future vintages too.

An English vineyard. About as different from Bordeaux as you can get.

The red harvest

While the whites were going through all these difficulties, the reds were generally looking much more healthy. Around 22 August, at the end of the hot August period, growers in the Médoc were saying that, if it didn't rain, the vintage would be an '89–'90 type. By the 25th, we were noting merlots at over 11° already, in spite of the size of the grapes, and, as in 1989, the acidities were low. At the véraison, most properties had planned to start the week of 8 September, but the end-of-August rain and especially that of 1 September changed their plans.

Some of the earlier-maturing merlots, especially on the right bank, suddenly got very fragile on the steamy hot day of 2 September, and had to be picked in a hurry a week early. These musts were rather weak, light and green. Later, we could see one or two such vats in many cellars, even on the left bank.

However, in vineyards that had been less fragile before the rain, the continuing September sunshine encouraged the bolder growers to push back the harvest. So, as September wore on, with the sun permanently out, the panic picking of 2–10 gradually turned into a more relaxed approach, as each grower had time to work out his exact ripeness programme for each parcel and to go through the vineyard, as for the whites, in several 'tries'.*

No one dared hope that it would not rain in September (as it had at the equinox on both the 1995 and 1996 merlots). Any rain like this would have been a much more serious problem in 1997: the 1995 and 1996 merlots were solid enough to take it, this was not the case for the 1997s. In addition, the nights were much warmer this year: 12–18° C, as opposed to the 7–13° C of last year, so any further outbreaks of rot would spread rapidly, and by now it was too late to spray. But the miracle happened: from 2 September to 5 October, apart from slight drizzle on 12 September, there was not a drop of rain. This is possibly an all-time record.* And, for the month, the maximum temperature was 2.9° C over the average. So, everyone could take their time to catch up the ripeness that had been so severely put into question earlier.

Most Médoc merlots were harvested between the 8th and the 19th, with some continuing on to the 24th. The right bank was generally finished on the 17th, with some continuing on to the 22nd. This was a totally different story from the 3–4 day merlot harvest of '95 and '96, when the ripening was so regular.

The cabernets took even longer. Although the grapes were large (they were often mistaken for merlots this year), they had resisted the rain, as always, very well. As usual, there were growers on both banks who wanted to get the vintage out of the way and picked far too early, often encouraged by the oenologists who were saying that the analyses were not progressing, that the vine had finished its cycle, etc. True, as during the rest of the year, the vine seemed more interested in developing its foliage than in ripening its grapes, and the leaves were still growing well into October, all perfectly green (except where the oidium had got at them). But of course the usual subtle transformations were in fact happening in the grapes, and some wonderful vats of late-harvested cabernet were made right up to 16 October. Some of these bunches had flowered in May. The average 'hang' (flowering to harvest) is 100 days. Such cabernets had therefore been on the vine for 140 days. This must be the longest 'hang' in history.*

The showers coming through with the cold-fronts on 6 October never caused any problems. On the contrary, they helped the final cabernets get to perfect maturity. The vine had taken on no water since 1 September and the afternoons had been continually over 28– 29°C and this light rainfall just sparked it back to life.

Down in Sauternes the final 'tries' were made right into the second week of November and some pickers are even still out today. The remainder of October was permanently fine from the 14th onwards, with cool Easterlies suddenly reducing night-time temperatures down to 3– 4°C. And on the morning of 30 October, the vine's leaves, green and fleshy on the 29th, were suddenly burned by a hard frost. Once more, just as it had been unusually olive-green in April, the vineyard took on another

strange colour, this time of russet-brown. There was no gradual change to yellow, just straight from green to brown. Those leaves had been green and vigorous for 220 days — it was quite clear where the vine's priority had been this year.

So ended the most bizarre growing season, and, just to show that the vine was not the only plant to get a bit lost in it all, the cherry-trees in Bordeaux grew a few blossoms — at the end of October.

1997: What kind of wines?

One: Dry whites. With so many different picking dates, spread out over such varied weather conditions, and with so much variation in growers' reaction to the irregularity of the ripening, no one can say that 1997 dry whites have any particular style.

The Pessac-Leognans have clearly produced some very successful semillons and some lovely fragrant sauvignons, picked before the end-August rain. But even here, the wines are very mixed in style. Some are ripe, rich and fat, others more elegant and finer. As a general rule, growers were initially disappointed by the absence of aromas, finding that the power drowned the fruit, but are now finding much more fruit-flavour.

The situation is similar in the straight Bordeaux Blanc appellation, where the most successful later-harvested semillons, if properly selected at picking, present the same characteristics of richness and fullness, with the fruit only now coming through. These wines are being compared to 1990 in style.

Earlier-picked sauvignons range from the weak, bland style of the hurried pickings of late August, to the remarkably fine-flavoured aromatic quality of the later harvests.

Certainly the proportion of really good whites will be very small this year, and the market will need to be very choosy, probably very quickly.

Two: Reds. Vinification: 1997 was a tricky vintage to vinify: because of the speckledy nature of the bunches, and of the size of the grapes, the great fear was that the colour extraction would be insufficient. The oenologists had generally given out the guideline of early harvesting, because of the rot-risk, and, as a result, they often advised short macerations, so that any green elements would not get exaggerated in the tannins.

With demand for straight Bordeaux Rouge once again in excess of current stocks, and each grower's '97 more or less assured of being sold, there seemed little point in risking the harvest just to gain a little extra ripeness.

So, more than in 1996, there will be plenty of light, rather green wines around, and the general average of Bordeaux Rouge is clearly less good than the '96. However, the more progressive properties, and especially those that are more export-oriented, looked after their vineyards properly during the summer, taking the trouble to snip out the rotten or underripe grapes and to control the foliage, and consequently were able to harvest at much more uniform maturity, and these have made some extremely solid wines, in some cases superior to the '95 and '96.

Higher up the scale, most growers went to extraordinary lengths to ensure maximum ripeness. The biggest problem here, therefore, was not so much the lack of colour as the temperature of the grapes as they came in, often at 29– 32°C. The must needed to be cooled immediately if the fermentations were not to start too fast. Many also kept the musts on their skins for some time, in order to obtain a cool pre-fermentation extraction. Because the grapes were so big, the juice-to-skin ratio was high and 'saignées'* were performed on most of the merlots and some of the cabernets, but in general not more than in 1996, because, with lower natural sugars in the grapes (typically 12.5° for the merlots and 11.5° for the cabernets), many were afraid of over-extracting the skins.

When the fermentations got under way, they were usually extremely fast and remontages* had to be implemented very quickly, very often with a tank-to-tank 'lessivage'* once or twice right at the beginning in order to capture all the good parts of the tannins right away. Thereafter, most preferred to go easy on the extraction for the rest of the fermentation, doing remontages lighter but more frequently than in 1996. For the same reasons, very few estates let the tanks warm up at the end as they had done in 1991 and 1992.

General characteristics of the reds
The result of all the above is that the general character of the vintage is of gentleness and finesse: as befits a less strong type of wine, the wines rarely appear forced. The merlots have great roundness of style, with a supple, soft texture that often recalls pinot noir. The merlots seem generally lighter and finer on the right bank than their more weighty counterparts on the left bank. The cabernet sauvignons and cabernet francs, as usual, had thick skins and have consequently produced some good firm tannic wines, especially in the later-harvested ones. However, because the grapes were bigger this year, they are less fat than the 1996s.

Overall, the red 1997s seem to be headed for a style that, in most cases, bears little resemblance to those hot over-mature vintages of 1989 and 1990 (which some had thought still possible at the end of August), nor do they have the aggressive roasted attack of the '95s or the dry nature of the '86s. On the other hand, they do not have any of the underripe cabernet qualities of the '88, a vintage which was frequently alluded to during September, nor of the vegetal qualities of the '78, the last really 'speckledy-bunch vintage'. The gentle nature of the wines suggests something of the '83s, with, here and there, more concentration than that.

General characteristics of the reds by region
By region, the differences are less evident than in 1996, when the left bank had totally drier late summer conditions than the right bank and consequently made stronger wines. In fact this year, the late August rainfall was the other way round: in the last ten days of August, Pauillac got 66 mm whilst St-Emilion got only 28 mm (Pessac-Leognan got 37 mm, Southern Graves got 43 mm and the Entre-Deux-Mers got 50 mm). However, the 1st September rains which were frequently the determining feature, fell all inland, the Médoc being almost totally spared.

Nevertheless, as in 1996, it was not so much a question of the amount of rain that fell; rather of the closeness of the rain to the harvest date. The more time the bunches got to dry out and concentrate after the rain, the better chance there was of making excellent wine (provided the grapes remained healthy). So St-Emilion and Pomerol were therefore once again penalized for being an early-ripening vineyard. In addition, they took the brunt of the 1st September rain.

The Médoc, on the other hand, picked their merlots and cabernets four to seven days later, and in addition, didn't get much 1st September rain. So the total period of dry weather before the harvest was sometimes as little as three days for the right bank and sometimes as much as sixteen days for the left bank. When we add in the greater proportion of late-harvested cabernets in the Médoc, we have to conclude once again that 1997 is more of a Médoc vintage, and to a lesser degree a Graves vintage, than a St-Emilion or Pomerol one.

Sauternes

The 1997 sweet wines have been remarkably successful, but at the beginning of September, it didn't seem that way. The region suffered from the April frosts, and the general problem of irregularity was aggravated by the subsequent counter-budding. In addition, the region had some hefty attacks of 'pourriture aigre'* during the summer, which had to be weeded out progressively. There was also some grey rot.

However. the 'trie' system that every serious vineyard around Bordeaux had to adopt exceptionally this year is just usual procedure in Sauternes, so it came naturally to Sauternes growers to tack on an extra 'trie' at the beginning in early September, to weed out all these problems. Generally, for a good-sized vineyard, this took two to three weeks, and since some good botrytis grapes* were found along the way, this became known as the first 'trie'. In most vineyards, it lasted well into the third week of September, and produced just a few hectos* of elegant, very aromatic semillons as well as sauvignons that came in at a very honorable* 17–20°.

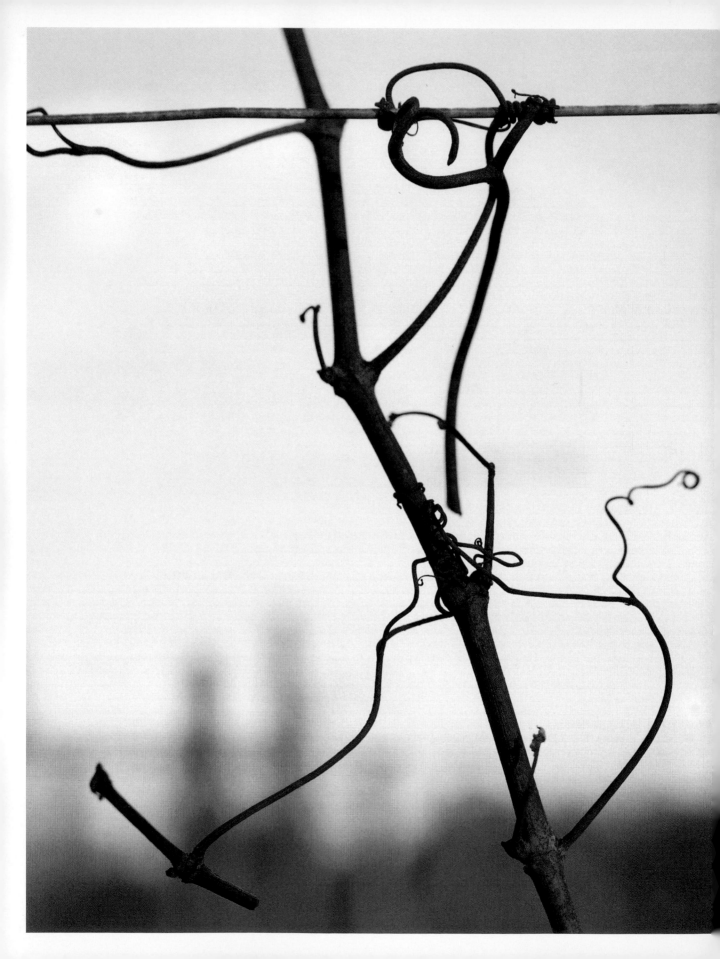

With the vineyard now cleared of all potentially defective grapes, the succeeding 'tries' could deal normally with each grape as it botrytized. At this time in 1996, it had rained, and the second and third 'tries' were not nearly as concentrated as the final mid-October ones. In 1997, it was the other way round: the weather remained constantly fine (apart from the 6–14 October light showers), and the middle 'tries' turned out to be the best. During this period, botrytis was widespread but, as in all Bordeaux regions, concentration was slow. The result was that as in the dry autumns of 1983 and 1988, the grapes got to the 'passerille' (shrivelled)* stage very fast. once they had botrytized. At that point, they have to be picked, and, since the vineyard was concentrating so irregularly, these 'tries' turned into a truly gymnastic vintage: the 'tries' were longer than in 1996, but the 'lots' inside those tries were much smaller, and the picking troops jumped around from parcel to parcel, as each lot became ready.

By 17 October, the best had been harvested. Many châteaux continued well into November, but by then the degrees had dropped and the results were not so good.

The 1997 sauternes will be more in the nervous 1988 style than the hotter-type 1989 or 1990. In most cases, it would seem to have more class and concentration than the very good 1996s, especially on the top of the Sauternes vineyard where the air circulation helped in the concentration process. The barsacs and lower-slope sauternes had more fragile grapes to work with, and have often made less full wines.

The sauvignons seem less concentrated than the 1996s (in which vintage everyone used a greater proportion), but they do not have the mandarin-orange character of 1995. The semillons are aromatic and full, maybe less fat than the '96s, but generally just as concentrated. Most came in during the middle 'tries' at 20–25°C in the top estates.

Yields are extremely low, often only 10–15 ho/ha*, compared to the '96s which had generally produced 15–25 (25 being the maximum permitted yield).

Yields

The official estimate for total Bordeaux production at 26 August was of 1m hectos white and 6m hectos red. After all the losses from imperfect grapes, the 1 October estimate was reduced by a total of 600,000 hectos. In the end, it is clear that volumes of all whites are extremely low.

In the reds, at the lower level, most growers seem to have 60 ho/ha and more, whilst at the châteaux, the figures are very erratic. One property made 60, his neighbour half of that. As a general rule, the top St-Emilion and Pomerol châteaux have produced a total of 40 ho, those of Pessac-Leognan only 25–30, while the Médoc is generally near the maximum, often 50–60 ho. These are figures for the total crop (Grand Vin and 2nd wine).

VINTEX. Telephone: 05 56 11 20 80. International + 33 5 56 11 20 80
Fax: 05 56 11 20 85. International + 33 5 56 11 20 85
17 November 1997.

*1. 'pointe verte' stage is the beginning of the development of the tiny grape bunch.

*2. 'vin de mars' — this does not mean a wine made in March but a wine from grapes which have developed early and so provided an early autumn or late summer harvest.

*3. 'Lune Rousse' — the Russian Moon is aptly named for the lunar phase which heralds frost.

*4. 'négoce' means commerce or trade but in this context specifically refers to those who trade in wine, *négociants* in other words, or wine dealers.

*5. 'Saints de Glace' — those saints whose name days fall when the risk of frost has, in all but extremely abnormal conditions, gone.

*6. Côtes du Ventoux — wine region in the north of Provence (Vaucluse) some 448 km from Bordeaux.

*7. 'des citoyens responsables qui savent prendre en main leur avenir' means they were responsible citizens who knew how to take their future in hand.

*8. 'nouaison' — vineyard work involving the tying up or the training of the canes of each vine.

*9. 'coulure' — a form of self-pruning exercise by vines in which the very small berries, a long way from becoming grapes, drop off. In moderation, this is a natural and unworrying process, though few wine growers appreciate seeing potential grapes disappear so early. In excess, coulure leads to a significantly lower crop.

*10. 'millerandage' — not always a circumstance to cause concern if it leads to smaller and more concentrated berries but often millerandage means disparately sized grapes in the same bunch leading to uneven fruit quality. In some advanced vineyards in the New World, smaller berries are more prized and millerandage a benign condition.

*11. 'Vinexpo' week — the important international wine show which Bordeaux plays host to every two years.

*12. 'oidium' is powdery mildew.

*13. 'mildew' is a fungal disease, liable to infect almost every wine region, and it is treated by the so-called Bordeaux mixture of lime and copper. Organic growers can officially use it.

*14. 'grey rot' is a fungal disease, the ignoble form of noble rot or *botrytis cinerea* which produces the world's great sweet wines, but unlike its noble brother the grey version is distinctly unwelcome and disgusting.

*15. 'pourriture acide' can only refer to grey rot or something like it.

*16. 'volatile smell' is literally the smell of vinegar created by bacteria attacking the juice of fungally damaged grapes — more or less grey rot again.

*17. 'véraison' is the start of the ripening cycle; it is the first stirrings of sweet things within the tiny, hard green grapes which will expand and soften.

*18. 'vendange rose' — picking when the grapes are pink rather than full-blown red.

*19. 'vendange verte' — picking when grapes are still green.

*20. 'analyses of the must at over 13° and total acidities of less than 5 g.' refers to the alcohol level of the must and degree of acidity measured at so many grams — it is not clear here, but not important in the context — of the amount of wine which would contain this level of acidity.

*21. 'aigre' bunches — that is to say sour or vinegary (and from which, as *vin aigre*, vinaigrette is derived).

*22. 'tries' — each passage of grape pickers through a vineyard is a trie and in dessert wine areas, where only those grapes affected by the fungus *botrytis cinerea* are taken, pickers would make several trips before all the affected grapes were picked.

*23. . . . there was not a drop of rain. This is possibly an all-time record.' An all-time record for Bordeaux only. In other regions, particularly Chile, lack of rain during harvest time and the period leading up to it is one of the reasons why the fruit is so superb.

*24. 'This must be the longest "hang" in history.' This is the history of Bordeaux. The 'grape hang' in Chile or New Zealand for example is also long and even in England the growing season has been extended by three weeks by the warmer summers. Obviously, the longer the grapes stay on the vines, and the more slowly they develop the nutrients sucked up from the soil, then, in theory at least, the more complex the finished wine.

*25. 'saignées' — bleeding off of juice to concentrate the final wine more fully.

*26. 'remontages' — the turning over of the cap of solid matter which forms like a crust on top of the must in the fermentation vessel, so that the juice is aerated and circulated. (Viticulturally, the term can also refer to the re-soiling of an old vineyard the earth of which has become stripped of nutrients or is exhausted; also used to refer to the replacement of top-soil in steep vineyards when extremely wet weather or stormy conditions have removed it.)

*27. 'lessivage' — leaching.

*28. 'pourriture aigre' — vinegary rot, grey rot.

*29. botrytis grapes — grapes which are beneficially affected by the fungus *botrytis cinerea*. These grapes go to make the great sweet wines.

*30. 'hectos' — an abbreviation of hectolitre, that is to say 100 litres. Also an abbreviation of hectogramme (100 grams).

*31. 'honorable' — American spelling in the original document.

*32. 'passerille' — shrivelled, apparently, though it's a new word for me.

*33. ho/ha — the amount of hectolitres of wine yielded by each hectare of vineyard.

I make no apologies for reprinting in its entirety such an illuminating and comprehensive report. It is certainly well outside my own expertise to have written such a thing and it gives a fascinating insight into the weather conditions which make one year's grapes so different from the next. It is true, I think, that in very many instances the location of a vineyard more even than its grapes provides the key to its aroma and flavour profile. As Peter Sichel, from Maison Sichel in Bordeaux, said in his 1998 Wine and Spirit Education Trust Winter lecture: 'a cabernet sauvignon from Bordeaux bears a closer resemblance to a merlot from Bordeaux than it does to a cabernet from Australia or Chile; as meursault and chablis are a better guide to the style of wine in the bottle than if both are labelled chardonnay.' Wise words. And in the context of the influence of the grape on the wine in the glass, fundamental to the understanding of wine's maddeningly delightful ability to surprise, astonish, and never to remain the same two days running, let alone for a year.

You only get out of a vineyard what you put into it.

Ten

10 Down to Earth

(All wine is, but is that what makes it taste that way?)

The Vintex Bordeaux report is not an unusual document — although so eloquent a statement of a year in a vineyard is uncommon. The French worship their soil. Bordeaux is a shrine. In such wine areas, the French concept of *terroir* reaches its apogee. *Terroir* is the lynchpin of the French 'brand'. It is, depending on your degree of cynicism, either a cunning ruse to protect real estate values or a proud extension of the French view of themselves which has developed since the revolution of 1789. According to this view, French is the greatest civilized language and France a nation of individuals each expressive of native regional soil and typicity yet bound by the common tongue and refined shared values. Monsieur Jérôme Quiot, president of the National Committee of the Institut National des Appellations d'Origine (INAO) which runs the Appellation Contrôlée system, has said, 'Ce qui fait le charactère et la typicité des vins AOC, c'est le terroir.' That is to say, what makes the character and typicity of wines appellated AOC is *terroir* — i.e., the dirt the grapes are grown in.

A nation of terroirists

For certain wine commentators, including me, there is a hollowness about the notion of *terroir* and AOC rules and they cannot stand up to any logical scrutiny. But for generations of wine drinkers the notion of *terroir* as represented by those sacred words on a wine label, Appellation Contrôlée, is nothing less than a badge of rank.

Terroir has been taken by wine drinkers as some sort of guarantee, conferring extreme quality on wine manifesting, or claimed to manifest, certain *terroir* aspects. In Bordeaux it has led to many wine names, individual châteaux as well as areas, being connected to the nature of the vineyard soil; Graves, as in gravel, is the best known but there are others. The notion is enshrined in French wine laws through the Appellation Contrôlée system and is the basis for many other countries' geographical wine laws. (In 1997, South Australia was the latest to fall in with this concept when it created the soi-disant Limestone Coast wine area which includes within it sub-regions such as Coonawarra and Padthaway.)

Soil, then, is at the heart of it. Soil, and what a romantic Frenchman once described as 'the call of it', is what is supposed to be found, detected by the nose and discovered on the palate, by the lavishly skilled wine taster. The highly developed nose of such a taster enables him to assign specific areas of production to various wines. Certainly types of soil and the composition of its rocks find expression in the wine and often define its style. However, there are so many other factors, as discussed in this book, which influence the wine that it is not always possible to know whether its taste is a result of the soil when it might be caused by other single factors and/or the accumulation of them:

One: The grape (or its clone).

Two: The wine grower's manipulation of the vines (the way the leaves are managed, type of fertilizer, pest treatments, the sowing of secondary crops between the rows, etc.).

Three: The winery practices (type of yeast, enzymes used, malolactic ferment, ripeness of fruit, blend of barrels, wood influence, etc.).

AOC regulations attempt to rationalize many of these factors (unlike the rules of Vin de Pays wines which are much freer and often result in more exciting, and much cheaper, wines). This is done so that variations, in theory, can be ascribed to the soil and the vineyard's location. But soil is just another way of characterizing a real-estate value.

Burgundies, red or white, and in certain great examples, have a distinctive smell and taste. A local expert might place the vineyard but it would be my contention that the soil of this vineyard would only be the determinant permitting the taster to identify the location in a few highly individual examples where particular mineral extracts are identifiable from having passed into the wine consistently over many vintages. This particularity which has passed into the wine is not, however, the same as extreme quality. It is merely difference and, compared to wines from other regions, the wine may be mediocre.

In any event, other factors came into play which, though detectable on the palate, cannot be accounted for exclusively by the composition of that particular vineyard's soil.

Many other French, German, Spanish, Italian and a few Portuguese wines have distinctive aromas and tastes, as indeed do wines from the Napa Valley, sites in Oregon, and Western Australia, Victoria and other Australian areas, as well as New Zealand, but although the makers will, in many cases justifiably, point to the soil as a contributor to this distinction it is subtle and hard to detect by any but these local noses. In instances when the subtleties are consistent vintage upon vintage, however, we can all recognize them. In some cases, it is a regional variant of climate and geography (such as a coastal location creating cool nights and so contributing to a particular acid structure). The reds of Rioja, the reds of the Alentejo in Portugal, whites and reds of Costers del Segre and Penedes in Spain, the whites made from the Albarino grape in Galicia, the whites of Friuli, the Rhine, Nahe and Palatinate rieslings, the whites of the Jura and Pouilly, Chablis and Muscadet, the reds of Cahors, Fronsac and Bandol, can all claim to have identifying characteristics which the mature and versatile taster will detect, enabling the vineyard's location to be named. But in none of these instances, and there are many others, do I believe that it is solely the composition of the soil, and the unique nutrients therein which find their way along the vines' feeding systems into the grapes, which we have to thank for it. Soil is an emotive, romantic, nebulous, illogical and seductive topic, and it is often of extremely ancient composition. We step in it at our peril; we must keep our wits about us.

A very personal list

With these reservations in mind, then, let us consider a list (a short one and my own very personal compilation) of certain of the world's wines which express, in my opinion, an individual aroma and flavour, and to each of which I will assign its soil composition and structure. Only the wine drinker can judge whether this means that these wines can only perform on the nose and in the mouth as they do because of these soils. I have an opinion on this, yes. It is that only very few soil structures provide a genuinely vivid and richly discernible difference to the general taster so that it is possible immediately to identify this soil from the wine. Where this characteristic seems to me a reasonable inference, it is indicated in the table which follows (which omits the huge number of variations which undoubtedly exist*). In other instances I would say that only a regional expert of many years' experience would be able to discern all the minor variances in aroma and flavour and be capable of ascertaining the area and/or vineyard.

The generalist taster, where a tiny arena is concerned, will not expect to tap such depths of deductive minutiae; but we can hope to develop our knowledge and broaden our palates to the extent that our ability to find the right wine for the food is enhanced and the depth of pleasure wine provides is enriched. This book has not been written for the competitive wine bore who relishes nothing better than spending precious conversational time with his nose in a glass fatuously trying to detect the precise vineyard before anyone else. My advice in dealing with creatures like this is immediately to show them the label, thus ending their agony, and then to show them the door, thereby ending yours.

* The variations possible here are akin to those faced by the intrepid individual who proposed compiling a complete history of every performed British play, only to realize that the project would end up comprising ten volumes of 1000 pages each. How else to cover every single play and its every performance? Where stands the written text in such an exposition? Hamlet, like cabernet sauvignon, assumes a different shape in different places and invites a different interpretation every year — yet Shakespeare's text, like the grape, remains the same.

A taste of the world's most soil-expressive wines

This list is very short and far from comprehensive. I have not considered that it is within my remit here, even if it was within the compass of my knowledge and tasting skills, to compare different vineyards from the same region (where known variations, due to soil, are claimed to be detectable on the palate).

If wine growers were to submit candidates for a definitive list on this basis, we would have several volumes. Wine makers, in Europe at least, regard soil as the defining characteristic of their wines. There are tens of thousands of vineyards in Europe. How could anyone list them all? On the other hand, the New World wine makers, by and large, believe that it is the wine maker him- or herself who most influences the wine. This difference in attitude divides the two worlds of wine, the so-called Old and the so-called New, but for the generalist wine taster, which most of us (in Britain at least) aim to be, these differences make an impact on the finished wine in ways which do not easily fit any pigeon-hole. In other words, we cannot compile a complete catalogue because the tastes of the vast majority of wines change, perhaps subtly but certainly discernibly, from vintage to vintage. Only with very distinctive soils, which appear in a particular wine's flavour structure year in year out, can a useful list, like the short one below, be attempted.

Various wine authors have tried in the past to ascribe certain tastes to wines of certain vineyards but only in 1998 was there a genuine geological assault on the subject via Terroir — the Role of Geology, Climate and Culture in the Making of French Wines by an American geologist, James E. Wilson. This interesting and very brave book is discussed in Chapter 17.

Red Wines	Region	Soil Structure	Smell/Taste
Aglianico del Vulture	Basilicata, Italy	Volcanic	Minerally: iron-y, earthy, stony
Comment: all red examples of this type exhibit this genuinely distinctive taste. Grape: aglianico.			
Barolo	Piedmont, Italy	Limey clay, sandstone	Licorice, tar, violets
Comment: Barbaresco, in Alba, is similar, though lighter — same soil and grape. Grape: nebbiolo.			
Bourgeuil	Touraine, France	Valley and plains: sandstone Hillside: tufa	Pencil slatiness, violets, raspberry
Comment: Chinon has much the same qualities. The cabernet franc grape does not taste so distinctive elsewhere in France or the rest of the world. Examples from tufa soils more austere.			
Châteauneuf-du-Pape	Rhône, France	Galets — big flat stones	Baked fruit/earth
Comment: the finest expression of this warm herby wine is not given to all examples. Often, outstanding wines from less well-regarded vineyards in the region, Côteaux de Tricastin, Rasteau, Gigondas, Vacqueyras, Lirac, Beaumes-de-Venise, also exhibit this relaxed, baked fruit/earth character.			
Chianti	Tuscany, Italy	Clay, limestone	Baked earth, terracotta
Comment: only the best examples, not the rubbish, exhibit discernible character. Grape: sangiovese.			
Coonawarra Cabernet Sauvignon		Red loam, limestone	Mint
Comment: chardonnay, riesling and sauvignon blanc exhibit a distinct mineralized quality here.			
Graves	Bordeaux, France	Quartz stones, clay, sand, iron oxide	Nutty, earthen
Comment: only an individual soaked in the style of these wines, which excludes me, would spot them.			
Priorato	Tarragona, Spain	Stony, slate and quartz	Nutty, pruney, bitter cherry, cloves
Comment: taste bolstered by high alcohol and rich tannins. Grapes: grenache, carignan.			

White Wines	Region	Soil Structure	Smell/Taste
Marlborough Sauvignon Blanc	New Zealand	Gravelly, with large pebbles	Grass, tightly controlled
Comment: arguable that soil created the herbaceous reputation of this wine — canopy management more likely the reason.			
Champagne	NE France	Chalk	
Comment: : pale soil equals no night-time heat retention so development of fine acids is enhanced. This finesse, however, is only discernible in the very finest examples of this wine.			
Sherry	SW Spain	Chalk	'off' flavours, salinity
Comment: the whiteness of soil means less warmth for the grapes, palomino, at night. Helps fine acid built up. However, whatever the soil contributes to the final character of the wine the unique yeast attack of the region, the so-called flor development, which is most noticeable as a smell/flavour identity.			
Moselle riesling	W. Germany	Slate	Mineral, acid
Comment: genuine soil composition makes the wines distinctive and special.			
Condrieu	Rhône	Crystallized silicated mineral soil	Apricot, sesame seeds
Comment: viognier grape grown elsewhere is apricoty, but only real Condrieu has the nutty undertone. This complexity is unique to this small vineyard region.			

11 The Game Wine Makers Play

(The secondary fermentation: it can be a primary sensation)

One of the elements over which the wine maker has control is the degree to which a wine, any wine, can enter its secondary fermentation stage. This stage, the malolactic, or 'le malo' as the French call it, may take place during the alcoholic ferment (but never before); it is customary, however, for it to take place afterwards.

'Le malo' is a bacteriologically influenced change of acids whereby the sharp, apple-like malic acids are transformed into the soft milky lactic acids. In established wineries, this ferment may take place without the intervention of the wine maker, but it can be induced and in new stainless-steel wineries it almost invariably has to be because there are no residual bacteria to stimulate it.

Most red wines in the traditional, old-established and cooler-climate countries require malolactic development otherwise they would be far too acidic. In some warm countries, white wines are restrained from any malolactic development whatsoever. White wine makers in general, and the makers of fresh young red wines such as beaujolais, will want to control or adjust the degree of malolactic development; just as it is possible to exercise power over the degree of alcohol, up to a limit which is normally but not exclusively around 15 per cent, which will be created when the yeast consumes the sugar, so it is possible to decide that 'le malo' will run the full 100 per cent, or half this, or merely stop at 20 per cent. In many New World wineries, different white wine barrels will develop different percentages of malolactic to provide the wine maker with another blending element from which to create a final finished wine. Malolactic fermentation sometimes inadvertently takes place in bottle.

What does this mean for the taster?

From the taster's point of view, the give-away clue on the palate (and the nose) to the influence of 'le malo' on a wine is diacetyl, which manifests itself as a butteriness of varying degrees of intensity. Australian chardonnay in the old days was so heavily influenced by diacetyl that it seemed possible to spread it on warm toast. Now the degree of malo is less, the diacetyl is a richly charming and comfortable component of the flavour mosaic of the wine and nowadays generally meshes more harmoniously with the overall acidity of the wine. Some wine producers abhor diacetyl. The most virulent opponents are, I suppose, the riesling producers of Germany amongst whom no degree of malolactic fermentation was ever dreamed of being permitted. However, the few so-called flying wine makers at work in Germany and a few native wine makers are experimenting with a degree of malo in their wines, not necessarily riesling but sometimes silvaner or blends containing rivaner, in order to re-energize the German wine industry's relationship with the UK wine consumer by making 'fatter' and, it is hoped, more 'New Worldy' and richer-tasting, fruitier wines.

Some New World wine makers religiously avoid malo. A particularly elegant Californian chardonnay can be produced, with the traditional richness of this variety as exhibited by this State's chardonnay vines (whatever the sub-region), and no malo be present. In Chablis, where 'le malo' is never sensed as a component of the purest style of this wine, the chardonnay grape can express, or certainly did so when I drank the Chablis of the 1950s and '60s, the most steely and gun-flinty fresh-edged of the various fruity guises in which chardonnay appears throughout the world.

Eleven

In the rest of Burgundy malo often, in older white wine of great finesse, expresses itself with a sour-butter or decaying hay aroma/taste and harnessed by the acidity, the toastiness of the wood and the other elements of the fruit, can produce a wine of compelling sensuality.

It does take some time for the taster to develop the knack of accurately estimating the degree of malo in a white wine. It often merges with the general woodiness of the wine, the richness conferred perhaps by some of the barrels in the blend being made from grapes picked a little later with even a degree of botrytis in them, and I know of no taster who can get it right, or indeed cares to, every time. (Botrytis is the so-called noble rot which concentrates sugar in dehydrated grapes picked late in the season.)

It's a tedious skill, malo detection, in the hands of the competitive male who likes to show off. But usually, wine makers are the best at accurately estimating the degree of malo, especially with wine they are regionally familiar with. If it comes from neighbouring vineyards and personally known neighbouring wine makers, the flavour and chemical profile of the wine's characteristics are firmly imprinted in their minds. The clues to an individual wine maker's style or 'signature' are always written most legibly for those in the same line of work.

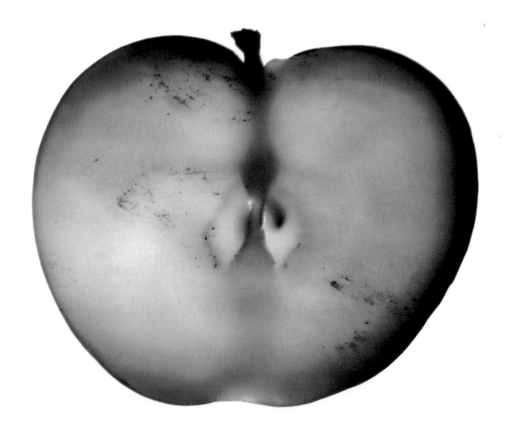

The old school.

Twelve

The modern school.

12 The Right School

(You can tell how a wine's been brought up by its manners)

Wood, when it is new and richly influential, is a wine's clothes. Not all wines require clothing. They can parade themselves naked; and certain of these, like a great steely Chablis for example or certain New Zealand sauvignon blancs, we applaud for their beauty in being so pure and free of the spicy cosmetic influence — coconut and vanilla, say — which wood can endow. Indeed, certain superbly crisp and clean unoaked chardonnays of Western Australia make many a much-vaunted Chablis seem distinctly flabby. Wood, as a flavour component of such wines, would be like fake sun-tan cream applied to an already beautifully olive complexion. And for wood read oak.

Oak is the favoured wood of wine makers, though other trees have been employed. In ancient times, palm and fir, by all accounts, were used; more modern choices include chestnut, poplar, ash and pine and even today a few Chilean wineries find a use for a local beech, quite beautiful in hue when made into furniture, called rauli. Oak, however, is the wood now considered to be the finest for wine fermentation and/or maturation because it is tough and watertight yet workable. It also contributes to wine flavours of its own which, in judicious and balanced amounts, enhance rather than smother the wine in a way no other wood can match.

The taste of oak

What does oak taste like? It can depend on the forest the oak grew in, firstly, and it depends on the degree of toasting (if any) the staves underwent. Barrels are all made over extreme heat and if steam or some other heating process is used to curve the staves then the inside of the wood may be left untoasted or, if toasting is specifically ordered by the wine maker (heavy, light or medium toast), this may occur over a wood-chip fire or some sort of electric contrivance.

Wood also influences the wine. It depends upon how long the wine is in contact with it. It is important here to understand that we are talking about barrels, not fermentation vats or storage vats which may be old, used many times, and have little influence over the flavour of the finished product. It is new wood, or partially new wood, that has the greatest effect on the smell and flavour of the wine which ends up in the bottle.

It is also true that wine which is fermented and matured in oak has a more ameliorated texture than wine which has been fermented in another container and then transferred to mature in new oak barrels. Chardonnays, and also other white varieties, seem to stretch themselves and become more committed woody wines when they have completed fermentation and maturation in the same barrel. There is fairly obvious chemistry at work here — the yeast has a part to play since it is still actively transforming sugar into alcohol in the barrel and the leaching of wood flavours into the busy wine is affected in ways which would be less profound if the fermentation was complete when the wine first met the wood. Highly skilled tasters may also detect the habitat of the ferment — entirely in wood, or stainless steel and then barrel transfer — from the richness of the flavour, its longevity in the back of the throat, and even the colour of the wine.

The paradoxical loss

White wine which is all barrel-ferment and maturation is actually paler than wine fermented in stainless steel and then transferred to barrel to mature. I cannot claim to feel greatly excited by the science involved and some wine enthusiasts are puzzled as to why it should be this way and not the other way round, but the fact is that when the fermentation solids in a wood-fermented wine are removed, some of the colouring matter has merged with these solids and thus does not pass into the finished wine. A wine from steel, racked free of fermentation solids, is embraced by wood and deepens in hue as a result of this contact and there is no subsequent dilution of colour. For the taster dedicated to a specific wine type from a particular region, it would, I think, be normal practice to spot the differences and draw meaningful inferences.

Oak by any other name

We can taste, and sometimes smell, the differences in flavour between wine aged in French oak and in American. A few experts can taste the differences in oak from the various national forests of France, though these differences are usually only a matter of differences in usage by the drinks industry of France since, for example, oak from Limousin enjoys a preference among cognac distillers because of its tannins whereas wine producers might prefer Allier or Nièvre. There is also German oak, Slovenian oak, Russian oak and a few others, but these are side issues of such an arcane dimension, except to a studious cooper, that we can ignore them. I am certainly not equipped with the knowledge or the breadth of experience to delve into this area. My experience is mostly limited to guessing that a wine has been aged in American oak rather than French and I have never seen much point in setting about acquiring the knowledge, even if I had the basic talent to begin with, to tell from which forest the oak was felled.

American oak, *Quercus alba*, is different from French oak, *Quercus robur* and *Quercus Sessiliflora*, from the taster's point of view because it is tighter-grained and less porous and thus has a detectable effect on the wine. The origins of Russian and Eastern European oak (Austrian, Romanian, Yugoslavian, Czechoslovakian) have been detectable for years in finished wine by highly experienced tasters and recent research by the leading French cooperage company, Seguin Moreau of Burgundy and Cognac, has led to some interesting results.

The main thrust is that Russian oak, in certain instances, is slightly superior to French — in that a panel of tasters preferred its influence — and so we may well, in future, be tasting more Russian influenced French wine (and no doubt that from other countries). Whether the drinker in the street will discern the difference I very much doubt, and reading the French research, which also includes physico-chemical analysis, I doubt whether anyone other than a cooper will find it a rewarding experience to worry about: the differences are obscure and very subtle (Russian oak seems to leach into the wine less methyl-octalactone, the woody aromatic component, so a subtler arboreal veneer on the wine is the result).

American oak, though, is a different beast with a fiercer set of horns. The taster needs to be aware of it. American oak is a more powerful influence on the wine, as many rioja lovers will testify since it is the rich vanilla impact of American oak, via the vanillins in the wood, on so many riojas that has for many drinkers made tempranillo a grape synonymous with vanilla, and even at times a coconut flavour, when in fact these flavours are almost exclusively a result of the American oak.

I sense that many open-minded young wine makers, however, believe that oak is becoming so expensive and fruit-masking that doing without it can be a positive benefit. It is true that many wines would not seem to be 'natural' (whatever that means in this context), without having been matured in wood, and to deny them wood would rob them of their legacy. However, if I were to be asked to forecast what will be one of the big developments in wine once the first decade of the twenty-first century is well under way, I would say a turning away from wood — even by the makers of fairly pricey and complex wines, perhaps mainly whites, sought by knowledgeable enthusiasts.

Take one teaspoon of oak essence . . .

Wood influences in a wine may also be achieved through refurbishment of old barrels. No one, as far as I know, is able to detect the difference except maybe the wine producer and — most certainly if he is also a serious taster — the cooper. Oak chips, small dice-sized squares of wood, and oak essence (liquid oak extract added to the fermenting must) are also means open to the wine maker, although the use of the second of these substances is questionable, not permitted in many regions, and, as far as I know, has never been used by a conscientious wine maker creating seriously delicious wine.

Oak chips, which are exactly what they say they are (linguistically, at least, a pleasant example of non-obfuscation in a jargon-plagued and often misty landscape), are less frowned upon. I have enjoyed certain southern French wines which have, without the knowledge of any local wine committee which would not have sanctioned their use, had their chips, and I've enjoyed wine in the 3-litre box which was most cleverly and agreeably wood-chipped. No honest wine which was intended to *bevin de garde*, that is to say, a wine to lay down in a cellar so that it could develop and improve over years, would be made using these techniques.

Wood spotting

For the taster, wood is fairly easy to spot as a shaping component of wine and the knack of recognizing it is not difficult to acquire. With practice, it becomes second nature. The two main oaks, French and American, influence wine in their various ways and in general it is the American which is less subtle and, if used clumsily, more fruit-masking. I have had the experience of smelling and chewing (via toffee-sized squares of wood which naturally resisted mastication) three sorts of oak — toasted to the same level as they would be by a cooper — used in barrel making. They were French, American and Hungarian.

The French simply had a woody smell which I was unable to relate particularly to oak, but the taste was of vanilla and caramel. The American had a huge butterscotch and vanilla aroma and was like a caramel toffee in the mouth. It was, for sixty seconds or so, not a painful experience (I resisted the temptation to swallow). The Hungarian oak lump was similar to the American one but with a more general woody undertone, that is to say twiggy and vegetal, and it had a hint of spice. But the overall impression was much flatter in flavour than the other two.

What does this tell us? The wood translates directly into the wine where the characteristics of smell and taste noted above are also detectable. We can all but ignore the Hungarian oak; most wines you will taste will be either American or French oak (with the Russians — helped by the French who have a commercial interest in developing Russian forests for cooperage purposes — coming up behind). The difference between French oak (from any forest) and American is broadly that the vanilla undertone — sometimes heavy — is a giveaway clue for a wine that has been barrelled in US oak.

The new broom. New World wine making techniques encourage greater pride in winery cleanliness.

It is interesting to compare exactly the same wine barrelled in different oaks. Here are four bottles of chardonnay, for example, all from the same Fetzer California vineyards, and of the same year, and the fruit in each case offers a different experience to the nose and the palate due to the differences in the woods. The chardonnay used in this experiment, from the 1997 vintage, was fermented with the same yeast and went through 100 per cent malolactic fermentation and, in every instance, the oak received the same medium toasting. The wines were tasted on 3 March 1998. In every case I could not tell from the colour which wine was which, so there was, to my myopic eyes at least, no difference between each oak in this area.

One: Barrel was French oak (from the Allier forest), made into barrels at Fetzer's own Mendocino cooperage. The aroma was barely oaky; being subtle it had to be searched for. But the taste was finely woody, not fruit-masking, and gentle. I could not say that the woodiness seemed specifically 'oaky'.

Two: Barrel was French oak (Allier) and made in France by the François Frères cooperage. The aroma of wood was slightly more intense. On the palate there was more evident woodiness, a gently astringent bitter/sweet feel, with a subtle vanilla hint and the wine was a more harmonious marriage of wood and fruit. It was possible to relate the fruit's woodiness to the taste of the same wood when I chewed on it as a chip.

Three: American oak, coopered by Fetzer Mendocino. There was an immediate sense of the aggressiveness of the wood on the nose. It was not pleasant. It was youthful and raw and suggested the wine needed much more time to harmonize with the wood. On the palate there was a long finish, much like the taste of wood as chewed on in the mouth, and this finish was not of fruit but of wood. Again, these characteristics all point to a wine in need of more time to develop and sort itself out — not in the barrel so much as when it is bottled and cellared for several months before being released for sale.

Four: American oak made into barrels by Tonnellerie de Bourgogne in the Napa Valley. This had something in common with number 3 above but was more sympathetic on the nose and the throat. Aromatically there was more lemon and decidedly more fruit on the finish of the wood. The wood was less aggressive than number 3.

This experiment was carried out with a handful of other wine tasters and journalists, and the overall impression of each of us was a unanimous preference, with the wine at this stage of its development, for French oak over American. It was interesting to taste also at this time a wine of which the 1997 specimen used in the test was a younger sister. This was the Fetzer Barrel Select Chardonnay 1995, a wine which had received 40 per cent malolactic fermentation, had spent six months in French oak, and several years in bottle. It had that fatness without blowsiness first-class Californian chardonnays exhibit, a touch of creamy softness due to its mellowing, and some elegance to its finish. It was evidently a French oak-influenced chardonnay. A bit of a dandy, this wine.

At the same experiment, I tasted some examples of 1995 Sonoma County Cabernet all of which had recently been taken from their barrels for the sole purpose of comparing the different oak influences. It was time, indeed, that the wine was bottled, allowed to lie for a few months, and then released. (In which context, it is important to realize that the finished bottled wine would be a blend of many different barrels.)

One: Oak was French (Allier) made into barrels by the Mendocino cooperage.
Rich, beautiful fruit with tannins and harmonious wood influence. A sweet oak spiciness was evident with a suggestion of mint. One taster present, Stephen Brook,* described the wine as having 'swagger' which is how I would have put it myself had I thought of it.

Two: Oak was French Allier, coopered in France by Seguin-Moreau. The wine had some of the characteristics of Number one but not in such complexity and developed richness. The wine was fruitier and simpler. It had more fruit 'sweetness'.

Three: Mendocino coopered French oak using a method designed to save money for the winery but still achieve genuine oak complexity. The barrel was four years old but had around eighteen new oak staves fixed inside. (These staves are not so much like the chips referred to earlier as pommes allumettes.) The wine suggested it was corked at first sniff, but it was then apparent that this characteristic was the coarseness of the wood. The taste was of raw woodiness, very young, arid and unattractive. The colour of the wine was lighter than number one.

Four: American oak barrel coopered in Mendocino. This seemed to me the best wine of the batch in spite of the excellence of number 1. There was a delicious sweet fruitiness, well-structured, a roasted coconut hint, and the wine was fresh and vigorous with excellent acidity. It was a superb food wine. The woodiness was a natural companion to the fruit and not an awkward partner. There was no suggestion of an aggressive US oak nature, although the roasted coconut undertone definitely gave the provenance of the oak away.

The conclusions to be drawn from this for the taster are that French and American oaks confer a different aroma and taste profile to the wine and are notable. For the wine maker, things are more complex. I do not think it can be readily inferred that there is a ground rule here; American oak may suit red wines of one vintage better, French oak white wines of another. The degree of toasting applied to the barrel is also a crucial factor, which may change from vintage to vintage. White wine certainly may be subject to a narrower choice of woods and toasts, due to the elements of its composition being fewer, but with reds there is an orchestra to conduct not just a string quintet to lead, and the judicious wine maker will surely keep all his or her options as open as possible.

Blending, using wine from different barrels, is obviously the key element with a single varietal bottling in a patchy or uneven vintage. For the wine maker, the time each wine spends in barrel is also a crucial point of judgement which will change from vintage to vintage. There is also the difference between the grape varieties. One red grape cannot be treated the same as every other. Again, the choice of which wood to use and the level of toast are vital.

Wine makers have 100 per cent control of nothing but their own temperaments. This is, unless there are unusually dramatic differences in sub-soil composition, what makes the wines of two neighbouring vineyards so dissimilar (you might say they have the same mother earth but different fathers to raise the fruit of it). They may be able to decide when the fermentation has stopped but they cannot turn the weather on and off during the growing season and they cannot make beautiful wine from ugly grapes.

Mr Brook is the distinguished and immensely readable author of books on everything from travel in New York and British Jewry, to the great sweet wines of the world and the sauvignon blanc and semillon grape varieties. Tasters with so wide a scholarship, catholicity of interests, breadth of tolerance and depth of style are in much better shape as individuals to see wines as they really are than the narrowly focused specialists to whom the wood, to employ an apt metaphor, is often obscured by the trees.

Thirteen

You never know what you're going to find in a bottle of wine until it's under your nose.

13 Spotting a Bad 'un

(Or how to smell a rat a mile away)

In Chapter 2, I went into the problem of wine contaminated by cork. This is a wine fault and so I must briefly return to the subject again here.

I do this because the detecting of faulty wine is often a tricky and poorly mastered skill — even by professionals. Not everyone can smell a rat, even when the malodorous creature is under their own nose.

I observed several self-confessed wine buffs, shortly before this book went to press, happily partaking of a bottle of St-Emilion which had been so contaminated by its cork as to make the wine as rampant on the nostrils as a ripe compost heap. I drank something else and said nothing, preferring to leave the wine's supplier, a generous and gentle man of otherwise wide cultural achievement, free of the embarrassment that the revelation that a bottle of his expensive wine was seriously ill would cause him.

However, when a corked wine is presented by wine merchants and Masters of Wine at a trade tasting, attention must be drawn to it. At both the London Wine Trade Fairs of 1997 and 1998 and the New Zealand Wine Guild tasting in 1998, I was offered corked wine from bottles which had had their contents sampled by others, apparently without comment, for at least an hour before I pointed out that the bottles were corked and the wine not in perfect condition. I am utterly baffled as to how any professional involved with wine can pass as fit a wine patently corked, and I am even more irritated that some of these wine trade professionals don't seem to care or have the gumption to do anything about it.

Are faults often seen as simply the character of the wine?

The wine trade has an annual competition to find wines worthy of awards and these are decided by a committee of expert tasters. Some 700 wines make the finals. However, the organizers of the competition submit all wines to scientific scrutiny, via the good offices and laboratory of a firm of analytical chemists and each year the lab discovers that an average of twenty would-be gold medal wines have faults. They are then eliminated from the awards. These faults are variously VA (volatile acidity which is discussed further along), too much sulphur (see later), or tainted with TCA (the cork taint discussed in Chapter 2).

Do these faults matter if experts cannot spot them at times? Of course they do. We are discussing subtleties here admittedly, but the buyers might be more discerning, given time to examine the wines, and feel disappointed. Surely the buyer of any new wine is entitled to a product in perfect condition?

Not all experts, we must conclude, are good at detecting certain wine faults. Many people, perhaps some of whom work in the wine trade, don't possess developed olfactory faculties. Indeed, from the research carried out at Yale University in America where human beings fall into three categories — super-tasters, medium tasters, and non-tasters — it seems likely that the smaller number of taste-buds possessed by the medium and non-tasters also implies a foreshortened sense of smell.

Any non-taster who wishes to detect faults in wine, therefore, labours under a serious handicap. The most important wine faults, as pure faults rather than stylistic mannerisms of a wine maker which might be termed foibles of construction, are detectable by the nose. This would not prevent such a person enjoying wine, but it might mean that an ability to appreciate subtleties was missing.

When a fault is perception, not reality: tartrate crystals

Wine faults detectable by the eye are few and, in one instance, not a fault at all but a perceived fault. This is a result of minute deposits of tartrate crystals, like particles of shattered glass in the case of a white wine, a reddish-brown in red wine, and in a developed tannic wine the crystals will be distributed amongst other richly sedimented material.

In all these cases the crystals can adhere to the underside of the cork and are made visible, disturbingly so to the virgin eye, as the cork emerges from the bottle. Tartrate crystals are not to be feared. They are the harmless residue of an important wine acid, tartaric acid, and although modern winery techniques can easily remove them with no objective other than to render the wine brighter and more pleasing to the untrained or easily offended eye, some wine makers quite rightly ignore such aesthetics. They prefer to handle their wine as little as possible (a consideration which may also stretch to barely fining and perhaps not filtering their wine before bottling). They assume, rightly, that the knowledgeable and passionate wine lover is more likely to reckon tartrate shards as evidence of a deeply caring attitude than the reverse. On this basis, my advice is to consider a tartrate deposit an ally of good taste.

Faults the eye sees for what they are

A muddy or hazy wine, caused by various things like **bacterial, yeast, or protein contamination**, is a crime in a wine. It is so rare a phenomenon nowadays, however, that I have only encountered it once in the past decade.

The other optically detectable fault is slight **carbon dioxide** gas in a still wine. This adds to the zip of many modern white wines and the gas is deliberately insinuated. It usually disappears as a visible phenomenon after some minutes in the glass, but the wine, the dryness of which its maker wished to counterpoint with a degree of zippy freshness, lingers — not unpleasantly in some cases. However, if the bubbles persist, or if they are ever noticed in a red wine, then I would consider the wine faulty and to be a candidate for exchange or refunding. You can rid a young wine of the gas, or certainly mitigate much of its presence, by repeatedly pouring it from one glass to another and holding each glass as high as possible. This gets air into the wine and it chases out enough of the gas to nullify its effects. The *pétillance*, the gentle sparkle, of young wine like Portugal's vinho verde is, however, a distinct and welcome characteristic and not a fault — though many examples of this often quite charming wine are anodyne and only rendered remotely thirst-quenching by the presence of the gas. Such examples are abominations and, since many are so light in alcohol as to be not much more potent than fruit juice, not what a developed palate would consider wine anyway. But I digress.

There is one other wine fault detectable by the eye. I came across it myself in a bottle of twelve year-old barbaresco offering itself for consumption while this book was being written. The wine had the most unhealthy **brown hue.** There was no need to smell or taste it to confirm the problem (which would have given the impression of balsamic vinegar to the taste-buds, and, to the nose, an obnoxious admixture of cider vinegar and the smell given off by a central heating radiator turned on after a season spent slumbering). The wine had oxidized, air had entered and had turned the contents to acetic acid with unabashed enthusiasm over a dozen years and the evidence of it was its extraordinary colour. The restaurant waiter who had

Chemical analysis of wine can discov̲e̲r̲ ... sters miss

Tartrate crystals — the average wine has less than this, but they still seem threatening.

brought the bottle instantly gave me a replacement and though the second wine was decidedly reddish-brown at the edge as it was agitated in the glass, this was consistent with a wine of its age and it turned on the palate with splendid maturity and seasoned fruitiness.

Line up and be counted

The identity parade of ten rogues detectable by the nose (and subsequently, in some cases, the palate) is as follows.

One. *Fault:* **sulphur.** *Detectable as:* prickle up the nose and the sense of slight 'fireworky' quality. It takes a few seconds but it gathers in the throat like the intrusion of acrid cotton-wool. Asthmatics are intensely susceptible to it and may gag. Indeed, at a lunch in Germany where I ordered a bottle of old sweet wine, one of our number at table was so overcome by the sulphur in the wine (an essential feature of certain low-alcohol sweet German wines since it prevents the high degree of sugar, still unfermented in the bottle, from re-fermenting in warm weather) that the paramedics had to be called and she spent two days in hospital. Sulphur is less prevalent than it used to be in the days of my wine-drinking youth and the event just related could not have occurred with a modern dry white or red of average alcoholic strength.

Two. *Fault:* **mercaptans.** *Detectable as:* reminiscent of onions or subtly burnt rubber and, since it is related to hydrogen sulphide (see below), it has a stinky edge to it. It can be created in the same broad way as hydrogen sulphide, and indeed is grouped within a similar chemical compound group, but olfactorily there is a difference between onion and a bad egg, as any curate will tell you, and so I have separated them as detectable wine faults. Mercaptan development is a later stage of H2S and often more insidious and difficult to counteract since it makes its presence felt not to the wine maker during wine making but to the wine drinker upon opening the bottle. Its removal, at this point, is impossible and time is no healer.

Three. *Fault:* **volatility.** *Detectable as:* sharpness, vinegariness, an unpleasant 'overripeness' of the acidic side of the wine.

Four. *Fault:* **2-4-6-Trichloranisole.** *Detectable as:* the stink of mushrooms, cardboard, decaying vegetation, uncleanness, mustiness, dusty-draweriness, old bookish/sockishness, and cobwebbiness. TCA, to which the chemical contaminant is abbreviated, is the most common cause of 'corked' wines and it is found in oak tree bark. At its most pernicious and wicked, it is rarely at one time all of the revolting things listed; most often it is not so rampant but simply a gentle assassin who kills the fruit. Many people, even tasters, cannot detect it in low quantities and may even consider it an aspect of a red wine's woodiness. TCA is a wine despoiler; a parasite which damages subtly rather than vandalizes brutally. By British retailers' estimates, between one in fifteen to one in twenty wines is corked. This is not the place for me to expiate at length on this *bête noire* — I have written and broadcast on the nuisance for some years and Chapter 2 of this book covers the problem in more depth — but it is a wholly reprehensible fault which sloppiness, by cork producers and wine merchants, is continually to blame. It is the reason why some wine makers would prefer to see their wines screw-capped and why many leading UK wine retailers are turning more and more to plastic corks which are genuinely neutral sealants. It is the existence of TCA which makes the necessity of smelling the cork the moment it emerges from the bottle the number one priority of every careful drinker or *sommelier*. If the cork smells of wine, or of nothing, there is little chance that the wine is TCA affected; if it smells musty, as it shouldn't, then the wine itself may be 'off'. I would say that in 70 per cent of cases where I have examined the cork and it has smelled fairly disgusting, then the wine is not as its best though it has not always smelled as unpleasant as its cork.

Five. *Fault:* **Barrel taint.** *Detectable as:* mustiness, a twiggy smell. To me, on the very few occasions that wine from tainted barrels has made it on to a UK retailer's shelf, it has been indistinguishable from the TCA contaminant referred to above. It is rare, and not to be confused with overwoodiness which is merely evidence of cackhanded wine making, often to be found in the past with barrels from American wood. Personally, I consider overwoodiness a fault, since it is a clumsy imbalance in the wine — certainly a flaw, though not a taint.

Six. *Fault:* **Acetaldehyde.** *Detectable as:* an 'off' odour, like fino sherry or certain vinegars but only in significant amounts. In a fino or other sherries, the characteristically developed edge of the wine is a deliberate feature of it and to be appreciated as such, but in a red or white table wine it is distinctly unwelcome. Certain white wines from the Jura in France also have this 'off' edge. With the development of modern wine-making techniques, the reductive technology of stainless steel where air is not permitted entry, it is unusual for acetaldehyde development to be in evidence to any appreciable degree. Indeed, it should be impossible; having said that, I have been told by one wine scientist that acetaldehyde is present in minute quantities in all wine since fermentation creates it, but it is not detectable by human senses.

Seven. *Fault:* **brettanomyces.** *Detectable as:* rats' tails. Not a very helpful metaphor? Try chewing on an old fur coat. You'll get the picture.

Eight. *Fault:* **hydrogen sulphide.** *Detectable as:* rotten eggs. This is an aberrant chemical monster born either of sulphur with yeast (mutating while the wine is on its lees) or nitrogen deprivation while the must is fermenting. It smells particularly uninviting, evoking one of humankind's strongest olfactory reactions — disgust, a wrinkling of the nose, and rising of the gorge — and it suggests, to the sensitive bodily defence systems, the presence of mild poison due to putrefaction and therefore cannot be tolerated. I would be surprised to learn that even those non-tasters with abnormally dormant olfactory thresholds would fail to detect raging hydrogen sulphide in wine. It is not common, however.

Nine. *Fault:* **volatile acidity** or **VA.** *Detectable as:* nail varnish or paint stripper.

Ten. *Fault:* **oxidation.** *Detectable as:* many of the things to which volatility is related (see above). Oxidation is most common either when the cork has developed a microscopic channel, undetectable to any checking mechanism or the human eye, which slowly permits air to get into the bottled wine and the wine slowly to decay due to the oxygen intrusion. In restaurants which serve wine by the glass, oxidized wine results from a bottle being opened hours or even days earlier: it has lost all its freshness due to the oxygen and become tart and insipid. Some wines can take being recorked or resealed and kept for a day or so in a cool place but these are usually sweet whites or odd specimens of a rich white grape, like chardonnay, which take on an added attractive quality to their fruit through being exposed to air for some time. But a fresh young wine should taste fresh and young.

It may well be that there are faults which no one has yet identified or correctly named. Certainly no human being can identify all the elements in wine or in grapes. As Geoffrey Taylor, analytical chemist, pointed out: 'There are 600 different compounds naturally occurring in wine. There are 400 compounds in grapes.' The fermentation and maturing process of wine, then, adds up to another 200 elements. Are all these elements entirely benign? Are certain combinations, at certain strengths, unfortunate? I'm not entirely sure that even Geoffrey, with all his sophisticated technology, would unfailingly be able to identify the lot every time he analysed a wine. In any event, do not all these mysterious compounds add up to form the wonderful complexity which is a wine — whether a straightforward £2.99 bottle or some richly conceived and mature £500 putative great growth?

Unforgettable moment: grape variety irrelevant.

Fourteen

Unforgettable moment: grape variety crucial.

14 The Unforgettable Moment

(How to cultivate a wine memory)

If you can't cultivate a memory, how can your cultivation of a taste for wine have a databank to call on? You will forget this week what you learned last. Faced with a 300-strong restaurant wine list, how can you find the most appropriate wine for the meal? Let alone one which might be a bargain? At the exalted level of a blind tasting, or at a tasting of scores of wines from a specific region, how will you remember which is which? How can you remember all those flavours, grape varieties, regions, wine makers, which wines go best with what dishes?

If it seems daunting, smile. You have already mastered and memorized an infinitely greater number of more complex and disorderly systems in order to have arrived at this section of this book. Memory is a doddle.

You just have to remember to memorize.

The reason why people forget is not because they have a bad memory. There is no such thing, clinically, as a bad memory except among sufferers of brain diseases like Alzheimer's. The more you use your brain to store information, the more the brain grows and is exercised to find ways to store things and to interconnect the retrieval systems. For isn't that what memory is, a storage and retrieval system?

If you don't put in, you can't take out

What does a retrieval system depend upon? Input. You can't get anything out if you haven't put anything in. That is why people say they have a bad memory; in actual fact all they have done is failed to store anything in the memory in the first place, or they have stored it in the wrong place.

To possess a really bad memory would mean not remembering you had a bad memory.

To begin to cultivate a memory for wine we need to examine two questions. First, what is it about a wine we most usefully need to recall? Second, what does such a wine share with other things which, in the normal course of our affairs, we commit to memory without trouble?

It is here that what was said about focus in Chapter 1 is very important. For one reason why many wine drinkers and indeed some wine commentators are less sure of their judgements than others is that they don't commit to memory the key information about a wine which makes them able to compare the one they are tasting with very many others they have tasted in the past. They will know lots of names of wine makers, grapes, regions and so on, but this is because *they felt these were important, so they took in the information in a way, often of course subliminal, which facilitated its easy retention and retrieval.*

My selective memory

Now, I can't teach you to develop a brilliant memory for wines (my own memory for names and faces is appalling and no trick I pull to try to rectify the situation works). I can, however, expand on and develop a few strands of thought which have undoubtedly helped me to possess a decent memory for wine and show how you might, by following a few ideas, develop one of your own.

Wine makers and wine commentators who specialize in or live in a narrow vineyard area, an appellated region of Bordeaux, say, or a designated vineyard conclave of south Australia, always manage to stagger us with their specific recall of their wines, their seemingly vast mental lexicon of grapes of the locality, and their latent ability to identify them. We shouldn't be so easily impressed but we are. Haven't you noticed how it is only these regional specialists who have such memories? I don't possess anything like their power of recall. It is not in my interests to have developed it.

This is because my focus is global and general: all wines, grown everywhere. This is why focus is the beginning of the development of wine-tasting skill because it is the fundamental building block which underpins memory. The regional specialist remembers because he or she is soaked in the locale and able to put a picture to every wine, an image to every taste, to press a trigger which sets off the precise bottle in question. In such a situation I am at sea. I can no longer be considered a suitable candidate to judge which of 300 McLaren Vale shirazes is most expressive of the region's soil and topology. Ask me to judge which of 300 red wines from fifty countries is the most richly structured, the best balanced, the most suitable for robust food, the most likely to age with distinction, and the best value for money, and I have no trouble. What is more, I will remember the majority of the wines which made an impact because I will have made notes and scrutinized the labels of each (if it was an open not a blind tasting), thereby causing a strong image of each wine to be created, usually via a dish which it will agreeably accompany, and thus easily stored in my mind.

Memory is based on imagery. The imagery is related to your tasting focus. Thus retail wine buyers are bad at coming up with a wine to go with food but brilliant at remembering similar South African sauvignons to the one under discussion because they tasted so many to arrive at a choice; wine makers are terrible at recalling the names of competitive wines which cost a lot less because they don't want to think about such irritations but they'll remember the precise second the hail came down in the vineyard at the harvest twelve years ago; and wine writers whose focus is value for money may have difficulty remembering the name of the wine maker because it is irrelevant.

What you memorize really interests you

If you're not interested in remembering something, you won't bother. In order, therefore, to remember wines you have to be very, very interested — whether you liked them or hated them. I have been quoted as saying that if I were to be shown 500 empties of wines I had tasted in the recent past I would recall the taste of each, its price, and which food it went best with. This is only partially true, since I would only remember the wines I liked best and the wines I found disgusting (if any), but undoubtedly the reason I could recall the wines would be because of the visual element involved. It is always easier to store an image than a word. A wine label, or a dish, or an aspect of the wine's character which can be visualized, is a storable image.

It would, I think, be possible for a person who wished to acquire such powers of recall to remember every wine he or she ever tasted simply by finding an image for each and storing it. It would have to have access to a retrieval system, like mine, which worked when presented with a wine list and it would be useful if it worked, unlike mine, when visiting various vineyards and recalling the occasions when the wines made there were previously tasted. I confess to being extremely bad at this. I simply haven't remembered the wines that way. I taste with other memory criteria in mind because of my focus; region of production and grape varieties don't get stored except in exceptional instances.

A never-to-be-forgotten anniversary: but will they remember the name of the wine?

Legion are the times people have approached me and tried to get me to remember a wine they cannot recall in sufficient detail, in order for them to buy another bottle. Their focus was too fuzzy or completely lacking; in order for them to have remembered the wine precisely enough they would have had consciously to commit its image to memory or write down its name. (Such a person, I might add, will often be able to reel off the name of every player plus substitutes of the football team he supports and provide the combination of different players of every crucial match in a season. Why? Not to have remembered would have been unthinkable.)

Sometimes I can remember the wine these people are after. I may have written about it. But often the wine is so loosely described as to be untraceable. These people will never make great tasters of wine because although they enjoy drinking it, they cannot interest themselves in it to the extent that it becomes important for them to develop a mental storage system of the wines they consume.

Become a wine writer — it's the only way to remember

I would propose to anyone seriously wanting to develop their memory, therefore, to make notes. Making notes by itself creates images, even more so if you write using visual images as reference points. This is the second step to remembering wines.

The third step is simply the retentiveness that comes by virtue of desire based upon need. How would you recall the way back to a hotel situated within a maze of winding streets? One way, short of a map, would be to fix in the mind certain key visual images at key points on the route. This involves a conscious memory process similar to that which allows students to remember key dates, royal successions, battles, and so on. For the wine taster, it does take practice over many tastings before the simple nature of key aspects of the characteristics of wines are remembered and thus differentiation and comparisons are made.

This third step involves progress side by side with the olfactory and taste mechanisms of the taster. Since these faculties are already cerebrally linked, via a nervous system, it is only a short hop to another part of the mind. You will be surprised how this develops as you progress and taste more wines. This is one of many reasons why I contest the academic dryness of the system of fruit similes which every wine student believes it is necessary to master in order to become an accomplished taster. This system is received wisdom amongst the great majority of wine writers and commentators, and certainly wine lecturers: under its fashionable diktat cabernet sauvignon is blackcurrant with perhaps a touch of bell pepper, sauvignon blanc is gooseberry with maybe a hint of grass, and the viognier grape is always apricot (but then so is tokay pinot gris). In many cases, of course, such fruity analogies leap instantly to mind when the wine is inescapably so endowed, but in many other instances the taster feels obliged to resort to overly stylistic fruit analogies because not to do so would illegitimize any claim to be a wine taster. Now, it is true that rose-petals and lychees are often discovered in gewürztraminer, grapefruit in schreurebe, plasticine or petrol in riesling, and when it is an honest, patently manifest aroma or taste, then some documentary use is served by the process. It also, of course, pins down why one likes or dislikes a wine via precise organoleptic impressions — that is to say, those features of wine the human senses can appreciate and catalogue (smell, taste, and so on). In this respect, the fruit analogy technique also has something to commend it.

But in encouraging the novice to adopt this technique rigidly, often against a natural inclination to find other aspects of a wine worth remarking upon (I myself find texture as

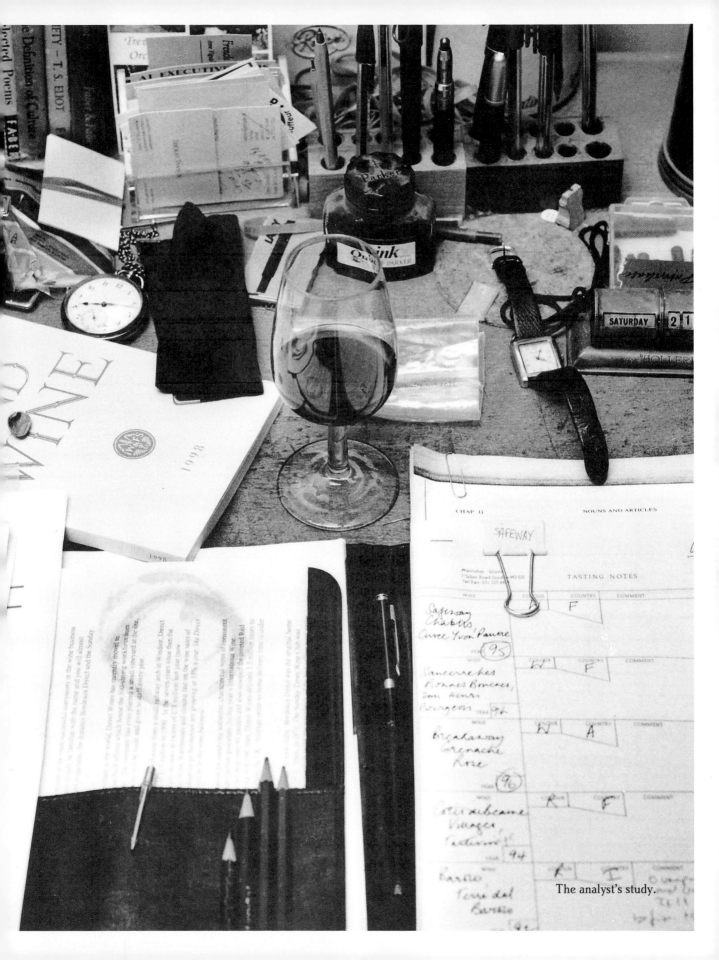

The analyst's study.

There are more memory cells in the brain than there are bubbles in 20,000 litres of sparkling wine.

Wine can leave an indelible stain on the memory.

important as taste, sometimes even more important, in some wines), this becomes the focus for the wine and so it is not remembered. Every wine does smell and taste of fruit, however quaintly, but often this grape-originated aspect is overridden by aromas and flavours of other things (rubber, smoke, vanilla, spices, wood, herbs, etc.) and thus there is pressure on the taster to find these. The current fashion in wine-tasting circles is to unravel yet more layers of fruity flavouring; like the emperor's new clothes, however, they may not exist in reality.

I confess I find much of this determination to discover such nuances in wines farcical. Many times at tastings a taster will remark to me something along the lines of 'Do you pick up satsumas in this viognier?' or 'Isn't there a suggestion of walnut oil in the flavour of this chardonnay?' and I realize that this taster's focus is so precisely oriented towards a systematic breakdown of a wine's aromatic and flavour components that for him or her to consider the wine as a value-for-money object for any likely purchaser, or to compare it with scores of similar-tasting and priced wines, or even to work out what food it might go with, are considerations out of bounds. If I am in a mischievous mood, I will often respond with a complete invention. 'No,' I will say, 'didn't get the satsuma. It was smothered by the paw-paw and the salsify.' Incredibly, many a taster will then proceed, upon examining the wine afresh, to discover exactly these characteristics in the wine even though I merely came up with the first fanciful fruit and vegetable to occur to me. Suggestion is a powerful incentive to find true what is not. This is why I prefer to taste wine unhindered by the opinions of others.

Be narrow-minded

It is for all these reasons that I believe it is difficult for most people to remember wines with any clarity or power of accurate recall. Their focus is so broad and analytical that no image can be summoned up which can be comfortably stored in the brain box and easily retrieved. Of course, the taster needs to consider the balance of a wine and the alcohol, sugar, acidity and tannin balance of the fruit (plus wood if it is a feature), and no wine can be reckoned good, ordinary or downright bad without assessing these things. But if the overwhelming aim of the taster is microscopic scrutiny of flavour components, perhaps even judging wines on their ability to exhibit such flavours, then the imagery which is the concomitant of good recall is fuzzy.

Overall, then, retaining wines in the mind is a case of reducing each to a vivid single characteristic which is memorable. Once this simple basis is established, much of the character of the rest of the wine (in my case, especially which food it will accompany, how much it costs, and usually but not always an aspect of its structure, like tannin) reveals itself even though you made no conscious effort to remember the detail. As you spend more time concentrated on tasting wine, the detail revealed as you sniff, gargle, and spit will be filed away.

When did you ever forget a memorable wine?

A wine which is memorable has made its mark. As with an unforgettable human being, a feature or a personality facet is the trigger for the rest of the character to reveal itself. If you want to remember wines, you will. If it is important to you to recall wines, you will do so. Once the habit starts, it's irreversible. Usually, you remember wine because the occasion was memorable; you drank an unusually delicious and rare sauvignon blanc at a dinner party, say. How can you forget such an occasion? It doesn't happen every day. But what if you could turn the tasting or drinking of all wines into memorable occasions? You'd remember all the wines. Just remember to remember and make notes. Every wine you taste will, with practice, offer up descriptive ideas as each is tasted. Every wine stands more chance of being mentally filed.

Memory is a filing system. If the wine isn't put in the filing system it can't be found. How do we file things? By orderly references.

After a while, if it matters enough to you, you will find a simple flavour/style analogy for every wine you drink. It will get filed away under that analogy and be capable of recall when you consult a wine list or look at wines on a shelf.

The more wines you drink the more wines you will remember. Happy thought, isn't it?

Is how long the wine lasts on the palate related to how long the wine lasts in the memory?

Michael Kluczko, who is wine operations manager at the Corbans wine company in New Zealand, remarked to me once how surprised he had been when he spent time with a champagne house in Rheims and discovered the emphasis placed on the base wine's persistence rather than initial flavour. 'They don't talk about flavour in a wine like we do or an Aussie would do. They discuss persistence,' he said, and went on to say that these French tasters actually used a stopwatch to time how long the wines, which would be candidates to form the blend of a so-called *grande marque* champagne, lasted on the palate. This is an interesting exercise. Undoubtedly, a memorable wine is affectionately remembered, sticks in the mind, because it persisted on the palate. The reverse is also true; many a horrible wine is unforgettable because it left a lousy taste in the mouth.

Many experts in the past have used stop-watches to see how long a wine persisted on the palate. Certainly, persistence is a characteristic of great wine. Any wine without persistence is unmemorable and can hardly be considered outstanding. A stop-watch race between several great wines to see which one lasted the longest, however, strikes me as an interest in wine carried to obsessional lengths.

A life dedicated to research.

How the other half decants.

15 The Oxygen Question

(Or why a wine is sometimes flat without air)

It is probable that the transferring of wine from a bottle to a fancy crystal decanter was not accomplished in the bad old days to improve the wine, but to impress those around the dinner table with the host's taste, moneyed life-style and sense of occasion. It gave the wine, as a servant poured it into a glass, a reverence which no bottle can quite convey. Decanted wine is wine in uniform; wine in formal dress.

True, the red wine drunk years ago by the upper middle and upper classes who were the only wine drinkers in those days, was mostly claret and port, was invariably old and had thrown a considerable sediment, and would have benefited from decanting, through a filtering funnel, to remove the bits. These bits would have been distressing to behold in a glass, especially for the ladies (so gentlemen assumed — etiquette forbade enquiry into the matter). This was an age which valued purity of surface to the reality of depth and thus the decanter was, and still is for some, a symbol of power, position, tradition and inequality. It is less necessary to judge of the liquid within a decanter than first to acknowledge and appreciate the degree of workmanship of the glass and the fineness of the engraving on the silver collar.

A question of taste

I incline to the view that the type of decanter a drinker wishes to use is totally a question of that region of taste outside this book's compass. There are various types of decanter, to be found not just in museums but on sale in the posher department stores, which claim to be perfect for sherry, whisky, gin, claret, red burgundy, port, etc., but the only one I personally have any time for is the port type. This is because vintage port is the only wine I would decant and filter a great many hours ahead; rarely more than a single bottle, the contents of which comfortably fill an old-style decanter. This can then be stoppered and forgotten about until the end of the meal or the following day in some cases. Elderly gentlemen — and I exclude myself from their ranks on two grounds — will say that I have ignored ancient claret here, but the reason is I very, very rarely drink ancient claret at home. If I did serve any I would certainly decant it, but I own no such wines.

Red and white wines, however seemingly grand, I transfer from bottle to large jug — at least an hour beforehand, if not two or three hours in the case of younger and more tannic reds. This container, with its big lip and open grin, is more of an invitation for guests to help themselves than wait for the white gloves of the butler to descend. All this begs a rather crucial question.

How long should a wine breathe?

Let me begin my answer (to a question I have been asked more than any other) by saying that though you may have noticed my aversion to jargon with regard to other aspects of wine tasting, this is an area where the jargon is not only unpretentious, it is accurate. Much of the vocabulary of the wine taster (such as the insistence that there is a technical difference between aroma and bouquet, when for most sane folk the words are interchangeable) is not designed to assist comprehension but obscure it or present unnatural hurdles for the lay-person. I make an exception for the term 'breathe'.

This is because it is not only an accurate statement of what is happening, it is also a dramatic way of emphasizing an important aspect of the presentation of wine in its optimum state. When, that is, it is most likely to show off its best attributes — and also reveal all its faults.

Breathing is the ingestion of oxygen. Air is life; air leads to death. Or rather air begins the process of the change of wine into vinegar, as acetic acid bacteria grow in the oxygen-rich environment of a wine exposed to air for hours, days, months.

For our purposes, before detectable decay sets in, air literally breathes life into wine — any wine. This is why large glasses enhance the drinking of it and why decanting, the pouring of the wine from the bottle into a separate empty container, can develop the wine and permit it to show us all its complexities and subtleties. By 'breathing' or 'letting a wine breathe' I do not mean opening it and simply letting it stand. This does nothing to aerate the vast bulk of the alcohol in the bottle, since only the surface is exposed to the air. It is a fallacy to suppose, and scientific research done in 1998 supports this point, that the mere removal of a cork lets a wine breathe properly. Air must get to the whole bottle. Decanting is the only way to get air into the wine. Decanting is not purely to do with the removal of sediment. It is to render the wine active for service.

It is not true that young wine is too raw to benefit from decanting or that white wines never require it. But experts disagree. I cannot concur with the assertion, which I hear stated now and then, that it is necessary to allow one hour of breathing for every four or five years of a wine's life. I would not under any circumstances follow this advice.

Nevertheless, we have it on the authority of a respected Australian wine sage, Mr Bryce Rankine (whose tasting manual is discussed in Chapter 17), that we should let wine breathe for one hour for every four years of its age. I question this arithmetic. On this basis, the 1949 Château-Puy-Lacoste (an underrated Pauillac property, cabernet sauvignon and merlot, whose wines have interested me for four decades) I toyed with buying, but did not, for a dear friend's fiftieth birthday in 1998 would have been opened fully twelve hours before being drunk. I couldn't find any 1948 wines I considered drinkable let alone affordable. Had I bought that forty-niner, however, and given it half a day's exposure to air the result would have been something approaching a wizened flop. A fifty-year-old wine, tannins fully ameliorated with the fruit and acidity (now perhaps getting floppy with age), should, in my view, be decanted and served immediately. I would expect such a wine to perform gloriously, if in good condition, for three hours and thereafter show its wrinkles.

Breathing and the age of wine often stimulate preposterous pomposities. There is no rule that would permit the age of a wine, any wine, to correlate exactly with an agreed time of breathing (which is taken to mean the removal of the cork, but which I always consider to be the time the wine actually spends in its separate container or decanter). I can think of thirty- and forty-year-old wines I have enjoyed, some not as hallowed as the Lacoste above, which had they been opened or decanted six or eight hours prior to drinking would have been well past their best. The advice that old wines need longer to breathe than young seems to be a metaphor drawn from geriatric athletics. It is not true, in every instance, of wine.

The inspiration of youth

Often, in fact, the younger a wine is, the longer it needs to breathe. This is especially true of immature reds where there is a degree of tannin. Young fresh, supple reds with little tannin will benefit from being poured into a jug and served instantly — particularly if they are chilled and it is summertime. With tannic reds, or middle-aged to older reds, it is advisable to check the

Let the air get to it.

decanted wine regularly, by sniffing, to ascertain its state of health. Tannin has no smell, it is true, but its presence does affect the nature of the fruit in the bouquet and a wine is ready when, from seeming somewhat austere and tight-fisted at first smell, it begins, after an hour, certainly after two or three, to show distinct aromatic signs of ripeness of fruit; opening up and displaying more vigorous signs of life, of generosity. This is a sign that the aeration has crept sufficiently into the tannin to have ameliorated it and made it softer to taste; it is in the nature of tannin to enclose the fruit, like a shell, and not only does getting air into the wine lift this shell or coating and make the fruit discernible to taste but its lifting also enhances the bouquet.

It is also important to add in the food element to this equation. If undercooked meat is being served, then by all means permit a strikingly tannic wine to be served after thirty minutes' or so decantation. If the food is at all spicy or richly sauced, then at least two hours breathing for a young tannic cabernet or syrah or chianti or rioja is a good idea. In general, little or no tannin should be in the wine, apart from wood tannin as with certain old-style riojas, where chillies are in the dish. With Indian spices, youth is paramount in the wine (just as the opposite is often true, I find, with the vintage of the Indian cook).

Some of the ancient wines which are purchased by collectors at auctions would, if opened following the advice of the hour-for-every-half-decade brigade, be almost rancid. A fifty-year-old claret, for example, is going to smell and taste as good as it ought, or as bad as it ought, within thirty minutes, perhaps an hour with a stubborn vintage, of the cork coming out. The only exception might be a legendary vintage of great claret, a distinction I would personally claim for my fugitive Lacoste, at the top of its form; such a wine would last hours in the glass and would develop greater sensuality as it gently respires — and expires — over three to five hours or even longer. (Why did I never buy that wine? I'll tell you. It was the price of two children's bicycles, a new stereo system, and five cases of Bulgarian cabernet sauvignon.)

Letting ten hours pass before drinking most old wines would be as cockeyed as waiting for your child to come of age before you read her a bedtime story. I've had old white wines go from smooth drinkability to wrinkled bitterness in twenty minutes; once the cork comes out of the bottle of such a wine you have sounded its death knell. Many collectors are simply amassing corpses, their cellars nothing more than necropoli, when they hold on to wine for so long that the fruit in the bottle will wither and die within a minute of the cork coming out. I have experienced such deaths with thirty-year-old sauvignon blancs and forty-year-old merlots. On the other hand, I once watched a pre-World War Two cabernet franc from Bourgeuil, opened in the 1980s, flow out of the bottle like a young athlete and taste perfectly fruity and delicious for the ninety minutes it lasted. This was a rare wine, however, from a personal cellar.

Finally, I must point out something about decanting wine — or rather, pouring it out of bottles and into large jugs as I do — which no other commentator on the subject has, so far as I know, ever mentioned. This is the curious fact that with no bottles on the table to distract the male guests (yes, it's almost always the men), with no labels to scrutinize or vintage dates to ponder over, conversation proceeds upon more open, more intimate, less stuffy and altogether more congenial lines. No man cares to guess what is inside the jug for fear of making a mistake; no woman does because it never enters her head to be so gauche. Everyone simply pours out the wine for themselves, another advantage of jugs; gossip and the interchange of ideas gather pace and pungency — just like the wine in the jug.

And, of course, if your wine has come, as many times does mine, from a supermarket and the name of this famous retailer is prominently displayed on the label, the use of the jug removes this advertisement. I don't consider the retailer's name as necessarily embarrassing, but it is blatant and I can quite see the point of view of someone who has gone to a great deal of trouble to prepare a dinner party preferring not to publicize the source of the dinner's meat and veg and/or wine. On the other hand, if the wine is superb you could argue that keeping it in its bottle might be seen to enhance the reputation of the host for shrewd purchasing without the sacrifice of quality. It depends, I suppose, on just who is coming to dinner.

Decanting restaurant wine

If you are arranging a special lunch and are going to splurge on the wine, then I see no problem in telephoning a restaurant where you are a known customer and asking them to decant a particular wine hours before you arrive. If the wine is faulty, the *sommelier* should have the wit not even to let you see it let alone serve it. I sometimes see, when I am eating in restaurants with outstanding wine lists, a customer ordering a wine which needs decanting for several hours to be at its best and I think what a treat is being missed by drinking the wine so early.

I also often ask for a restaurant wine to be stuck in a jug, especially young Chilean reds, which the *sommelier* would not in the normal course of events consider a candidate for decanting. The wine is better for the aeration. And this is true not just of reds but also of many young, and old, whites.

Mr Michael Brocklehurst, quartermaster or 'cellar man', as he calls himself, to the thirsty yachting community of the Côte d'Azur (via a company called Vins Sans Frontières Group) told me that he decants all wines for twenty-four hours before serving them at home and thinks them all the better for it. This was especially true, so he said, 'of the Rasteau you recommend in your TV programme, which I purchased locally' — Mr Brocklehurst is based in Saint-Paul-de-Vence in Provence — 'and which had so much tannin that it was different wine altogether after sitting in a decanter for a day.' Although Rasteau can be a notoriously tannic wine due to the local habit of not destalking the grapes prior to pressing so that even more tannin than is normal leaches into the juice, I'm not sure I would go quite this far. Perhaps the atmospherics of the Provençal littoral demand it. I certainly wouldn't like to treat a fresh, young, juicy Australian red to a twenty-four-hour decanting, but as with everything else in wine tasting, personal enjoyment is all. (And on second thoughts certain juicy Aussie fruit soups might well acquire some real bite after being let out for a day.)

Sixteen

From grapes to glass — is it a journey you can undertake alone?

16 A Class Act

(Some suggestions and a warning about wine tutors)

I am that monster of depravity and unresolved drives: the autodidact. I have never had a formal lesson in wine nor did I ever consider doing so when the liquid first touched my lips and entered my digestive system. I soon discovered, however, that it had penetrated to my soul. The seed of my gradual apotheosis into wine writer was planted in 1964 by the experience of first tasting real food with impactful wine and the pleasure this love, this union has given me has never lessened; on the contrary, it has increased.

I have been, then, untouched by wine appreciation theory except where it has been born and nurtured by by own instincts. I may regularly drink in company, may indeed in my own and others homes encourage conviviality, but my findings on wine I keep largely for my readers. I'm not the clubbable sort anyway, especially in regard to my enthusiasms (I make an exception for tennis).

I have never considered that the acquisition of wine knowledge and lore is an opportunity to score points, to enter into jousts, to show off, to humiliate wine waiters, or to flash a mysterious and possibly seductive language at credulous individuals or a paying audience. My interest in wine was purely to achieve a simple end: to acquire a delicious liquid every time I wanted a bottle and to find in it great joy as a drink and as an appropriate accompaniment to whatever food was in the offing. When I became a wine writer I simply translated that interest into a newspaper column and later an annual wine guide. I have been able to write this book because wine has been my constant companion for thirty-five years. I have read widely on wine and food but I am not a wine teacher.

But others are, or claim to be. I include below the names and addresses of individuals and organizations known to me as existing, but as to the prowess of the great majority I cannot comment. I have never seen any of them at work, apart from Christine Austin whom I specifically asked to appear in the BBC-TV series *Gluck, Gluck, Gluck* because of her down-to-earth, sympathetic approach to the subject.

I think it is only right and proper that I should make it clear that I am an impossible student whose temperament and personality are self-driven and motivated purely by their own perspectives. More reasonable human beings may find in any of these teachers a deep and limpid tributary of flowing knowledge and insight. I include every individual and organization whose existence has been made known to me but I cannot comment on the skill of each because I have experienced none. Doubtless I have committed the sin of omission and left out someone of true worth whose absence is regrettable.

As a general rule, I would avoid any teacher whose speciality is a mutant birth from a vinous passion which has to be funded by so-called teaching. Such teachers regard pupils as buttresses for the frailties of their own egos and on the evidence of the unscrupulous personalities of some of the people I met years ago who were, or claimed to be in those days, professionally involved in the dissemination of wine knowledge, I suggest you steer well clear of them. The wine world still has a sprinkling of mountebanks who, in making their offerings, are little more than Barmecides;* the nourishment to be found is illusory, only self-sustaining, and largely pretentious. I do not know if any of these persons also have pretensions to teach.

How will you recognize a good wine mentor?

One: First, ask what this person's favourite wine is. If the reply makes you smile with pleasure, you should be on *terra firma*. If the reply is wishy-washy, affected, touches the realms of the impossible, makes you yawn or leaves you confused, you have a huckster on your hands.

Two: Second, ask if you would get your money back if you were not satisfied or felt you were getting lousy value for it.

The quality of the answer to this second question, which isn't necessarily yes, sorts out the deadheads and the dandies from the true dedicatees. A good teacher will have fielded the question before and be sympathetic to offering an adequate, if not entirely watertight, response. The obvious place to start the list is with a Trust dedicated to wine education.

The Wine and Spirit Education Trust,
Five Kings House, 1 Queen Street Place, London, EC4R 1QS.
Tel: 020 7236 3551. Fax: 020 7329 8712.

This says of itself that it is 'the trade's recognized wine and spirit educator for more than twenty-five years'. The Trust has over the past few years 'welcomed an increasing number of amateur wine enthusiasts to examination courses'. Events are organized for people 'not wanting to study for a wine qualification, but who are passionately interested in wine'.

I fully approve of the Trust's aims and of the certificates which members of the wine trade, from supermarket wine department personnel to higher flying managers, study to acquire. I know little of the nature of these courses, but they boost confidence and instil knowledge because I've seen their effects on shop-floor staff. I can't say my own confidence, in other areas, has always been boosted by the WSET. For some considerable time, it sent me press releases with the name of its head office printed as Kive Kings House, but this quibble aside, the novice may learn much from a WSET course. Though having said that, I have not always been impressed by WSET indoctrinated wine waiters (one of whom once told me that she been taught never to smell a cork before presenting the wine to a customer!). There are three-day summer schools which include food and wine matching (always an essential skill to acquire). These are not cheap but far from outrageously costly. There are also food and wine workshops in the evening at very reasonable rates. Some courses feature quite rare wines. The acquisition of a WSET qualification is also possible in other countries:

Australia
Edith Cowan University, Pearson Street., Churchlands, Perth 6018.
Adelaide TAFE, 20 Light Square, Adelaide 5000.
Loftus TAFE, PO Box 926, Sutherland, NSW 2232.

---

* *The word comes from the* Arabian Nights. *A Baghdad prince of the Barmecide family invited a begger, Schac'abac by name, to a feast but presented him solely with empty plates and dishes. The starving wretch had the humour to go along with this cruel jest but finally received his just desserts. A similar happy outcome will not, however, befall the pupil who becomes entangled with the barmecidal wine tutor.*

Waiting for the grapes to ripen.

Waiting for the sniffers, swillers, slobberers and spitters to arrive.

Bahamas

Butler & Sands Ltd., PO Box N-51 Nassau, NP.
Bahamas Hotel Training College, PO Box N-4896.

Canada

Independent Wine Education Guild, 19 Grenadier Road, Toronto, M6R 1R1.
Dubrelle French Culinary School, 1522 West 8th Avenue, Vancouver V6J 4R8.
Kwantlen University College, 12666 72 Avenue, Surrey, BC V3W 2M8.

France

Lycée Viticole et Agronomique de Macon Davaye, 71960 Davaye. This centre coordinates courses run at *lycées* in Bordeaux, Montpelier, Orange, and in Alsace.

Hong Kong

The Wine School, PO Box 44239, Shau Kei Wan.
The Wine Institute, Room 2102, 21st Floor, Wilson House, 19–27 Wyndham Street, Central.

Ireland

Wine Development Board, 33 Clarinda Park West, Dun Laoghaire, Co. Dublin.

Japan

Ecole de Creation, Hasegawa Tower, 2-17-55 Akasaka, Minato-ku, Tokyo 107.

Malta

Institute of Tourism Studies, St George's Bay, St Julians, STJ 02.

New Zealand

Auckland Institute of Technology, Private bag 92006, Auckland 1020.

Sweden

Restauranghogskolan, Maltidens Hus, Soralsvagen 2, S-712 60 Grythyttan.

USA

International Wine Centre, 231 West 29th Street, Suite 210, New York 10001.
Rio Suite Hotel and Casino, Box 14160, Las Vegas 89114.

Zimbabwe

Hotel and Restaurant Association, PO Box HG 306, Harare.

Assocation of Wine Educators
63 Strand on the Green, London W4 1EN.
Tel/Fax: 020 8995 2277.
Contact: Philip Macgregor

For a reasonable sum — fifty quid before this book went to press — AWE offers a course in wine tuition which attempts to teach the appreciation of 'classic vine varieties as well as the factors which affect the different styles of wine'. These are called Grape to Glass workshops. The course consists of five once-weekly two-hour sessions in London and the cost includes wine, a glass, tasting notes, etc. There is also a one-day course.

The Association was started in 1994 and has around two dozen or so members who present wine courses. 'Each AWE member has his or her own personal presentation style and combines an experienced, professional approach with genuine enthusiasm,' said Ms Wink Lorch, one of the four original founder members. Wink, a most approachable person, has a phone number: 0181 670 6885. The unstuffy but authoritative approach of this bunch is summed up by their slogan which is 'Swirl, Sniff, Slurp, Spit'. The members are scattered around the country: Glasgow, Edinburgh, York, Liverpool, Birmingham, Bristol, Exeter and Plymouth. Contact them and they will send you a brochure and list of wine presenters. I do not know all of these AWE presenters but some I have found sympathetic in conversation are Phil and Christine.

Contact: Phil Cooper, 112 Hoppers Road, London N21 3LH (Tel/Fax: 020 8886 0304) and Christine Austin, 3 Greenwich Close, Rawcliffe, York YO3 6WN (Tel: 01904 612107).

Michael Schuster
Winewise, 107 Culford Street, London, N1.
Tel: 020 7254 9734. Fax: 020 7249 3663.
I am not acquainted with this renowned wine teacher who runs his courses from the basement of his house. He is not cheap, but his expertise was expensively acquired and he does offer, I suspect, as much value for the beginner as does the British School of Motoring (that is to say, that just as BSM will teach someone who knows how to drive how to pass a driving test, Mr Schuster may well be able to teach you how to taste even though you know full well how to drink). From what journalists who do know something of his methods tell me, he is a twinkle-eyed traditionalist who also knows value for money when he smells it. He is on record as saying he is opposed to the fruit-salad school of wine writing and that sounds good to me (even though I am a fruity writer myself).

Majestic Wine Warehouses
Odhams Trading Estate, St Albans Road, Watford, Hertfordshire WD2 5RE. Tel: 01923 298200. Fax: 01923 819105.
This wine retailer has organized occasional tasting events outside of the ones which regularly take place at branches (which merely revolve around half a dozen wines being opened without tuition). At these more ambitious events, a wine grower or maker will ususally conduct the tastings of his own wines plus wines from the same region. The cost is very reasonable with regard to both the quality of the presentation and quality and breadth of the wines. These events are very irregular.

Heathcote School of Excellence
Jacksons Row, Deansgate, Manchester M2 5WD.
Tel: 0161 839 5898. Fax: 0161 839 5897.
E-mail: CookerySchool@Heathcotes.co.uk.
Contact: Andrew Lee
This establishment's eponym (Paul Heathcote) is known to me through his restaurant cooking, but as for the quality of the school's wine and food evenings I cannot comment. They organize wine trips and wine courses for beginners.

Lay & Wheeler
Gosbecks Park, Colchester CO2 9JT.
Tel: 01206 713522. Fax: 01206 769552.
Contact: Sue Wheeler
This wine merchant runs regular courses in wine tasting, wine and food appreciation and matching, and is a recognized training centre for the WSET courses. They run workshops, tastings and courses, some of which call for a dress code of jacket and tie. (Tip: make sure you carry a tie clip; it's embarrassing if you spit all over your new Paul Smith silk tie. Or, like the smarter male gynaecologists, instead of a tie wear a bow-tie.) Over the past few years there

have been specific events on riesling, the so-called super-Tuscan wines (pretentious gobbets of fruit masquerading as great bordeaux), wine and cheese, Portugal, Germany, the wine glasses of George Riedel, and individual châteaux and wineries. One evening involved the attendees being regaled by the 'reflections on wine, travel and life' of Ronnie Corbett, the comedian. You could do a lot worse...

Bibendum Wine Limited
113 Regents Park Road, London NW1 8UR.
Tel: 020 7692 2720. Fax: 020 7722 7354.
Internet: http://www.bibendum-wine.co.uk.
This is a very professional and versatile wine merchanting operation, importing wine for supermarkets, selling cases to restaurants, as well as flogging the odd bottle to any individual who cares to drop by. They run a constant series of hedonistic programmes in which opulence and fun are the keynote rather than stuffy education. No one could fail to learn something from regular attendance at these events which have featured, for a fair fee, such things as the rising stars of the world's merlots (plus mystery celebrity guest), the Rhône, California, champagnes, whites, burgundy, as well as restaurant-based events. None of these comes cheap but then neither do the wines on display.

Institut Français
17 Queensberry Place, London SW7 2DT.
Tel: 020 7838 2144 and 020 7838 2167
(where the direct contact is Tanguy Dagorn).
Philip Macgregor (see AWE above) lectures here and prices are extremely reasonable and cover all the regions of France. Classes consist of up to forty people (hence the prices) and each session, one a month, lasts about two hours. The cynic might say this is all part of the French government's programme to spread the culture of their country, but so what? Once you've mastered France there's only Spain, Italy, Germany, Hungary, Romania, Bulgaria, Malta, Portugal, Corsica, Sardinia, Switzerland, Luxembourg, Moravia, Moldova, Greece, Turkey, Russia, Croatia, Macedonia and England and you've got most of the wine-growing countries of Europe bagged.

La Reserve
56 Walton Street, London SW3 1RB.
Tel: 020 7589 2020. Fax: 020 7581 0250.
Contact: Anne Whitaker (Tel: 020 7978 5601. Fax: 020 7978 4934)
A wine merchant not afraid to have an introductory 'How to Taste' programme (around £30) progressing to much more ambitious tasting, hosted by wine writers and trade gurus, where the great growths of Bordeaux are quaffed (sorry, tasted).

The Wine Guild of the United Kingdom
The Vine House, Rookery Lane, Broughton, nr. Stockbridge,
Hampshire SO20 8AZ.
Tel/Fax: 01794 301 784.
Contact: Jeremy Bennett
This was formed in 1985 to 'promote the knowledge and understanding of wine within the UK'. Until I came to write this book I had never heard of it. It says it provides scholarships to wine waiters. I hope they teach the blighters about cork taint and wine variation. I am unaware of any wine courses that the Guild runs for the non-professionally employed wine enthusiast.

Arblaster & Clarke Wine Tours

Contact: Lynette Arblaster: (Tel: 01730 893344. Fax: 01730 89288)

This specialist operator of wine tours has a large itinerary of holidays involving wine regions with, so it says, 'experienced wine guides'. I have no experience of this company, nor do I know of anyone who has. But you might it find it useful to check out what is available, even though it is in the nature of these things not to be cheap. However, approached studiously this sort of travel might be an agreeable way to learn more about the wines and the wine regions in which you are most deeply interested. Travel broadens the mind, so we are advised to believe, and it certainly deepens the palate.

Decanter Fine Wine Encounters and Masterclasses

Tel: 020 8774 0616 (Hotline — which may change).
Fax: 020 8781 0550.
E-mail: BILL@LHM.CO.UK

The inspiration behind this operation is *Decanter* magazine, a publication for those committed to wine. The last one to come to my notice involved various experts (e.g. Michael Broadbent of Christie's, Serena Sutcliffe of Sotheby's plus wine producers) explicating a defined set of wines — grand cru rieslings from Alsace, for example, or vintage port — during one single ninety-minute so-called masterclass. Leaving aside the sloppy terminology here — for the term masterclass refers specifically to those already fluent in a discipline acquiring even greater insight from an acknowledged master — this is an expensive way to acquire only a superficial amount of knowledge in a limited amount of time: £28 for ninety minutes was the ticket price in November 1998. The well-heeled wine buff will lap it up; those who simply, and in fine hedonistic spirit, wish to swill so-called Great Wines will also enjoy the experience. Anyone who keeps their wits 100 per cent intact during such tutoring tastings cannot fail to learn something. However, the publicity material for these 'masterclasses' claimed that the event was 'The Greatest WINE TASTING ever' from which the intelligent sceptic will surely learn something of importance before even a glass has been raised.

Wine Courses for Chefs

Run by Enotria Winecellars and *Harpers* wine magazine. **Tel: 020 8963 4820**

Enotria is a wine importer and sells a lot to restaurants. *Harpers* is a wine trade magazine. The aim of the London-based course is 'to focus on the practicalities of restaurant dining, rather than abstract rules of food and wine matching'. The courses — six sessions in each course — revolve around guest chefs cooking meals and a wine tutor discussing the accompanying wines. A degree of hearty eating and genuine drinking seems to underpin the idea here. Anyone who likes to socialize with a cheerful and unpretentious bunch of imbibers, and is in the restaurant business, would find these courses of some value.

17 Tasteful Tomes

(Which books are worth putting your nose into)

Paradoxically, the more one drinks the drier one's taste becomes but the more one reads the sweeter one wants the text – well, certainly where I am concerned. By this I mean that when you first get the taste for wine and along with it the thirst for knowledge, you consume just about everything that comes your way. Then, discrimination begins to set in and you sift more thoughtfully and search more assiduously for real juicy sustenance. Never has this been so true in this day and age when so much rubbish is written and published about wine and food, so many jejune stylists pen arid banalities, and gimmicks abound.

The past ten years, keeping pace with the spread of wine drinking in Britain, have seen an explosion in wine books and myriad pamphleteering; whereas when I took my first hesitant steps it wasn't so much balderdash and codswallop I had to wade through as elegantly overwritten, highly strung histories of the vine in France or Germany, loads of irrelevant quotations and *fin-de-siècle* memories and fantasizing about a long-lost age.

It wasn't until Hugh Johnson came along in 1966 with his seminal book called simply *Wine* that the mould was broken. His was a voice and a passion to which the wine drinker in the sixties, a revolutionary decade in so many other respects, could immediately relate. His prose was a cold sharp slap in the face, invigorating and fresh, after the stale proximity of so many tediously clinging cobwebs.

In 1997 alone I received twenty-two wine books (I do not include wine guides or atlases in this) for review. I would say only one (see *The Wild Bunch* by Patrick Matthews) had any merit, individuality, insight and real freshness and deserved a place in the intelligent drinker's contemplations as he or she relaxed in an armchair, the book in one fist, a glass of wine in the other.

For those wishing to learn more about wine or just wanting to enjoy a well-written appraisal of a certain aspect of wine or a region or the opening up of a genuine original wine-drinking mind, the fruits are meagre. But they exist. There are interesting books on wine worth having and my selection of the most persuasive known to me follows. Some may not be found on your local bookshop's shelves without prior ordering, but they are the ones I think most worth your while to look at. I cannot claim unreserved admiration for each of these books but where I do have a quibble I say so. I have not included out-of-print rarities or uncommon titles, but only books published over the recent past which should be obtainable without going to a huge amount of trouble.

Books on wine tasting

Pocket Guide to Wine Tasting by Michael Broadbent (Mitchell Beazley)
First published in 1982, and revised and brought generally up to date several times since, this is a genuine pocket guide which also fits the beginner's need to go step by step, firmly yet gently. Mr Broadbent is an urbane stylist, makes no unnecessary demands, and he makes his points with aplomb and precision. It covers areas not touched on in this book, notably the making of wine-tasting notes, wine-tasting glossaries, certain regional breakdowns and vintage considerations. His view of wine is lofty. He is a senior employee of Christie's wine department and is hugely knowledgeable about fine wines (and the auctioning thereof). Anyone organizing wine tastings will find areas here I do not cover.

The Taste of Wine by Emile Peynaud, translated by Michael Schuster
(2nd edition, John Wiley & Sons, 1996)
First published in French in 1983, this is the most internationally respected book on, as its subtitle says 'The art and science of wine appreciaton'. Professor Peynaud is an academic at the Bordeaux Institute of Oenology, has trained

over 1500 wine makers and scientists, and is consultant to the poshest châteaux in Bordeaux and vineyards in other countries. It is an excellent translation into English, this book, and anyone wishing to take their wine-tasting expertise on to the level at which it can either become professionally oriented or more classically grounded, must at least look into Professor's Peynaud's mind via this book and get a glimpse of his authentic authority. It is systematic, rigidly consistent in its logical and scientifically based conclusions and arguments, and if it has not been thoroughly read, or at least skimmed, by every seriously ambitious wine maker and wine professional in the world I would be very much surprised.

Tasting and Enjoying Wine (A Guide to Wine Evaluation for Australia and New Zealand) by Bryce Rankine (Winetitles, Adelaide, 1990)
Useful little tome, if not without opinions with which I cannot agree (as touched on earlier in this book), and speedily written. Its best use is for serious wine evaluators since wine faults are covered well, as are the techniques for serious wine appraisal by analytical logging and scoring.

Books on countries and wine regions

A Concise History of Australian Wine by John Beeston
(revised edition, Allen and Unwin, 1995)
Australia has yet to produce a vinous biographer (James Halliday excepted) to match the rich tones of its wines, but this is a useful book which provides a good overview of the development of the vine on the world's largest island. It is not a wine guide.

The Wines of New Zealand by Rosemary George
(Faber and Faber, 1996)
Easily the best book written on the phenomenon which is New Zealand, written by an English individual with a strong grasp of her subject and wine in general. She was not a specialist in the region when she began researching the book, though she surely is one now, and she is never a limp or anodyne apologist for the wines. There is a lot in the book and the reader will get a lot out. I would only quarrel with the book's first sentence: ' Meteoric' implies transience and NZ is, I think, going to be with us (as Ms George herself would doubtless agree) for as long as wine is drunk.

Wine Atlas of Australia and New Zealand by James Halliday
(Angus and Robertson/HarperCollins, 1991)
An invaluable book to which I refer often. It is well written, well designed and well researched.

Wine Atlas of California by James Halliday
(Angus and Robertson/HarperCollins, 1993)
Stuffed full of solidly researched enthusiasms and, like his other atlas book, essential for anyone with an interest in the region. Mr Halliday has gravitas plus a sense of humour.

'Angel's Visits': An Inquiry into the Mystery of Zinfandel by David Darlington
(Henry Holt & Company, New York, 1991)
An enthusiast's guide to one wine type, true, but also stuffed full of interesting information about vines and Californian wine and its personalities. I guess, like me, you have to really love zin to want to read the book, but it is not so parochial as this implies and its insights, including many about wine tasting (and Robert Parker among others), are myriad.

Vino: The Wines and Winemakers of Italy by Burton Anderson
(PaperMac, 1987)
Somewhat out of date now, but a tremendous book on the most complicated and impossible-to-classify wine country on the planet. Gallops along a dusty trail gallantly and expeditiously with very many revealing and fascinating encounters with wine growers from every region in Italy.

'Life Beyond Liebfraumilch' Understanding German Fine Wine by Stuart Piggott (Sidgwick and Jackson, 1988)

Goes into the cellars of all the great German producers and the result is a must-read tome for anyone interested in wine development, wine history, and the individuals who make riesling the greatest underrated grape in the world.

French Country Wines by Rosemary George (Faber and Faber, 1990)

An essential guide to the lesser-known wines and regions of France, written well and pertinently organized. It is only a pity that Faber could not or would not publish the book as originally written, which was considerably longer and more detailed; but this would, at a guess, have meant either publishing it in two paperback volumes or directly in hardback in an expensive edition which might have put it beyond many readers' pockets. Still, it is an essential book for anyone wishing to meet some of the wines and several of the makers who fall under the title's vast umbrella.

Bordeaux by David Peppercorn (Faber and Faber, 1991)

Exactly what it says: a compendious château-by-château listing and evaluation of Bordeaux's wines and its regions. Goes into history, ancient and modern, and is authoritative and comprehensive.

The Wines of the Rhône by John Livingston-Learmonth (3rd edition, Faber and Faber, 1992)

A magnificent and unrivalled guide to the wines, vineyards, growers, *négociants*, wine practices and problems of one of the world's most compelling regions. Solidly written, excitingly so at times, superbly researched and well organized.

Burgundy by Anthony Hanson (2nd edition, Faber & Faber, 1995)

It is doubtful if any living creature knows more, cares more, is so objectively knowledgeable about this region and its wines and wine growers as Mr Hanson who in addition to his enviable, wine merchant-based expertise and enthusiasm writes well and entertainingly. He is also authoritative and critical; no soft option, however temptingly proferred, is taken, and the book is essential reading for understanding burgundy as a wine and as a geographical (almost metaphysical) expression.

The Wines of Alsace by Tom Stevenson (Faber and Faber, 1993)

Erudite, comprehensive, detailed, no vineyard stone is left unturned by the relentless Mr Stevenson in this excellent overview of this region, its vineyards, hundreds of its growers, and its wines. As an organized document on a wine region, nearly 600 pages long, it is exemplary in its detailed listing and ease of reference. An essential reference work for the taster who enjoys Alsatian wine.

Grand Vins: The finest châteaux of Bordeaux and their wines by Clive Coates (Weidenfeld and Nicolson, 1995)

A vast work of love and scholarship, passion and pertinacity. Mr Coates covers all the great, and not so great, classified growths of all the regions and provides details of each château's wines and vintages over a long period. A truly exceptional work of devotion and drive from which it is impossible not to learn something.

Côte d'Or – A celebration of the great wines of Burgundy by Clive Coates (Weidenfeld and Nicolson, 1997)

Ditto everything I said about Mr Coates's Bordeaux book. It is exhaustive and exhausting. Like a splendidly rich fruit cake, you can only nibble at it. But it is immensely rewarding and hugely educative about the region and its wines. Each of Mr Coates's two books is a pilgrim's progress and thus the author's faith in the miracle of French wine is implicit; in this regard agnostics may find the cake hard to chew in places.

Terroir – The Role of Geology, Climate and Culture in the Making of French Wines by James E. Wilson (Mitchell Beazley, 1998)

The first and only wine book to my knowledge to be written by a professional geologist. I was fascinated by much of the geology but the book is padded out with wine history, much of which is not germane, and one suspects that

South Africa: soft wines, rugged landscape.

the publishers urged this extra burden upon an author who has enough on his plate with soil. Only very occasionally, and then only partially, does the book do what I wanted it to do: to contradict my belief that it is the wine maker who makes the wine and not the sub-soil. What it does not do, and perhaps could not do, is to relate the structure of every vineyard soil to the taste of the wine and thus prove that AOC wine laws are based on an immutable truth. It is impossible to deny the importance of sub-soil, and this book is special in that respect, but I just wish it had not just scraped the surface of its premise. It is also a pity that the geology is all French. What about the geology of the world's most significant vineyards elsewhere? But, all that said, this book will teach you loads of things even though the tone is reverential and accepts received wisdom as to the superiority of France as a wine producer.

Guide to specific wines

The Wine Buyer's Guide by Robert Parker (Dorling Kindersley)

A periodic updating and listing of wines, some 7500 of them, from all the world's major wine regions by the world's most independently minded outsider and systematic taster. He is an outsider in the sense that he works for no one but himself and his adoring readers who fall on his every word and follow religiously his meticulous rating system, especially when that system awards wines 90 points or over out of 100. He is a grand writer, though given to stylistic muddiness and ambiguity at times, but he is passionate, unstuffy, and he knows his own well-stocked mind. He upsets lots of people. I have never met him, and hope I never shall; I say this because on the old Roman principle that no man is a hero to his valet I prefer to preserve my heroic illusions — as I would *mutatis mutandis* if given the heavenly chance to meet Marilyn Monroe — concerning this wine taster and I do not wish them shattered, perhaps, by meeting someone who is, or certainly was, a member of that much loathed species of mankind, an American lawyer. I hope Mr Parker lives and drinks forever and continues to insinuate his thorns into wine regions' sides. No other wine guide comes close to his. My own, in comparison, are as mackerel to the whale.

Encyclopaedias, glossaries, histories

The Oxford Companion to Wine, various authors edited by Jancis Robinson (Oxford University Press, 1994)

Essential to have this encyclopaedic, multi-authored volume which delves into everything about wine from abscissic acid to Zweigelt. Over 1000 pages of authority, insight and very up-to-date information written by a phalanx of authorities of whom the most lucid and least peripheral (and the most absorbing) are the academics and the scientists.

Vines, Grapes and Wines by Jancis Robinson (Mitchell Beazley, 1986)

A splendidly comprehensive, elegantly illustrated and well-written book — indeed superbly tightly written and unflinchingly well-organized for so massive a subject as the world's wine grapes. It is an essential book for the taster who wishes to advance his knowledge of hundreds of grape varieties and where, how and why they are grown, and with what result. It also has, certainly on the original cover, by far the prettiest picture of this attractive woman, who is rarely done justice by photographers, for it captures her soft-focused romanticism along with her hard-headed grasp of wine and her ambition to prosper by communicating its mysteries.

The Story of Wine by Hugh Johnson (Mitchell Beazley, 1989)

The history of wine, extensively illustrated, from its beginnings to its current state by a man with a grasp of a fluent and unclichéd pen.

The Art and Science of Wine: The Winemaker's Option in the Vineyard and the Cellar by James Halliday and Hugh Johnson (Mitchell Beazley, 1992)

It covers the whole systematic making of wine and vineyard practices, is well and pertinently illustrated, and not the least bit stuffy or pretentious. A very useful book.

Discursions and excursions (or an interesting mind opens up)

Wine Snobbery: An Insider's Guide to the Booze Business by Andrew Barr (Faber and Faber, 1988)
This book received more writs than any wine book in history yet after the dust settled, and certain amendments were made, we were still richly entertained by an iconoclastic and lively individual to whom, I may as well admit, I owe more than to any other wine writer. (It was Mr Barr who inspired me to get my bum off the ground and get back into a bicycle saddle and I am greatly indebted to his example.) This is not strictly a taster's book, true, but it touches on many things from the dubiety of chaptalization (adding sugar to increase alcohol) and other additive practices to the scorching of the hides of certain sacred cows.

Drilling for Wine by Robin Yapp (Faber and Faber, 1988)
The man who, as the dentist who inspired the title, first introduced me in early 1970 to the obscure wines of the Rhône. Mr Yapp is now a successful wine merchant and this is a fascinating ramble.

The Wild Bunch: Great Wines from Small Producers by Patrick Matthews (Faber and Faber 1997)
I include this book because not only was it the only one which really grabbed my attention during a barren year, 1997, for such publications but because it is so personal. I have doubts about the advisability of its pseudo-wine-guide dimension which dates the book immediately when in fact it is a stroll, more timeless in its findings than any specific bottle guide, through certain wine regions. It recounts meetings with small wine growers and other feisty characters, presenting as it ambles along an eclectic panorama of prejudices and predilections. I could not, however, as I picked my way through this amiable book rid myself of the suspicion that Patrick was a little too keen to ingratiate himself with a critical élite and thus I worry he might too quickly become a cobwebby old bore unless some enterprising publication doesn't snap him up as its wine correspondent and set him a brief to upset some apple carts.

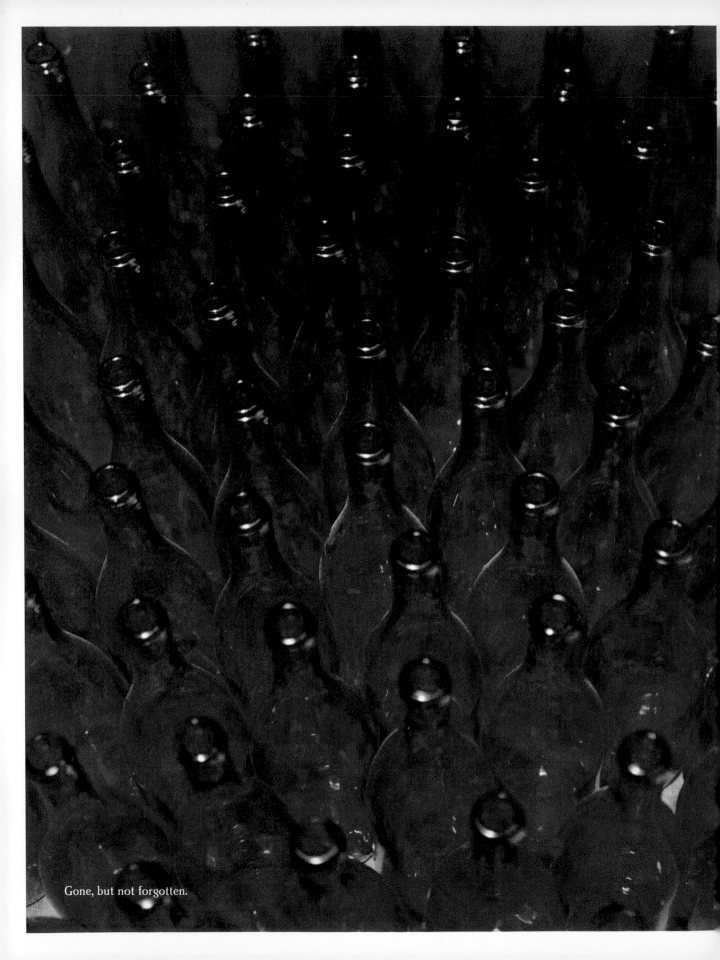

Gone, but not forgotten.

Eighteen

As bottles grow in size they acquire various wonderfully exotic names: Magnum (two bottles), Jeroboam (4 bottles), Methuselah (8 bottles), Salmanazar (12 bottles), Balthazar (16 bottles), Nebuchadnezzar (20 bottles). The taster will detect subtle differences between the same wine, aged over years, from different sized bottles because the bulk of alcohol will cause each bottle to develop differently and acquire a measure of individuality.

18 A Glossary of Terms

I have tried to write as friendly a book as possible, but its subject has a scientific basis. Scientific terms, then, are impossible to avoid since they refer to a specific phenomenon for which no other linguistic reference exists. I include tosspot, hardly scientific but nevertheless carrying an exact and widely misunderstood meaning, for reasons of elucidation and to return the word to the world of wine where it belongs.

Acidity Sharp, appley, tart — call it what you will, acidity is sensed by the taste-buds as a bluntness counterbalancing the sweeter fruit element of a wine. Acidity preserves and permits maturation. Wine makers use a scale, pH so called, to measure acidity levels in wine; the higher the acid the lower the pH figure.

Aldehydes This embraces a group of chemicals which make themselves known when oxygen mixes with alcohol. For the taster, these form two sorts of sensation: the withered sense of raisiny, perhaps almost rancid, maturity found in sherry, and the grassy, leafy characteristic, called herbaceous, which denotes the presence of what is called a leaf aldehyde.

Anthocyanic Refers to the chemicals responsible for forming the colour of a grape.

Botrytis Full name is *botrytis cinerea* and it is the so-called 'noble rot' or fungal disease of grapes. To be avoided if straightforward wine is the idea but if a sweet rich wine is desired then botrytis will dehydrate the grapes, concentrate the sugars, and lead to deep, honeyed flavours.

Bouquet Strictly this does refer to the complexity of a mature wine's odiferousness and is not necessarily interchangeable with aroma which, for some authorities on wine, relates to the specific odour characteristics of the grape variety. There is something to be said, so purists claim, for this argument; we wouldn't refer to a grape having a bouquet, we would say it had a smell. If one accepts this idea then it may also be easier to swallow the concept of the somewhat fanciful word 'bouquet' as meaning the full range of smells of the wine in its fully mature state. A wine which has been influenced by wood, air, and the wine's chemicals changing over time.

Brettanomyces A yeast. Usually avoided at all costs in winery. Its effect is described in Chapter 13.

Diacetyl A chemical compound found in wine. See Chapter 13.

Esters Formed in two ways in wine, these compounds are aromatic (see Chapter 13). Esters occur during fermentation and develop as a wine matures.

Glycerine/glycerol Fermentation produces these viscous, sweet chemicals.

Hydrogen sulphide See Chapter 13.

Macération pelliculaire French term for the time, and technique involved, during which wine is in contact with its skins.

Malolactic ferment ('le malo') Wine enjoys a double fermentation. One transforms sugar into alcohol, and is called the alcoholic fermentation, and the other, if the wine maker permits it, transforms malic acid into tartaric acid. See Chapter 11.

Meniscus The perceivable edge of the wine as it touches the inside of the glass; it appears different in hue to the mass of the liquid. In a white wine the meniscus may appear colourless; an older red will shows an orange or brown tint to its meniscus.

Mercaptans See Chapter 13.

Mesoclimate and microclimate These terms are often misapplied. A mesoclimate refers to an area from as large as a single vineyard to a group of several and is different from the regional, or macroclimate. Microclimate is that which appertains to a single row of vines, or even a single vine, or a designated portion of a vineyard.

Must The pressed juice of the grapes on its way in a fermentation vessel to becoming a fully fermented wine.

Oenological In its broadest sense means the studying of wine and comes of course from the Greek word for wine. Nowdays, an oenologist is a wine maker.

Organoleptic Refers to any aspect of a wine which impinges on the senses of smell or taste.

Oxidation What takes place when wine mixes with air.

Pétillance The gentle ripple of carbon dioxide bubbles, not as in a full-blown sparkling wine, but in a wine which is only slightly gassy, like a vinho verde.

Phenolic An all-embracing set of chemical compounds. Anthocyan (see above) is one.

Photosynthesis The process whereby a vine, or any plant, converts sunlight into sugars via its leaves using branches as the delivery channels to the fruit. This is a huge and very green subject, rather vital for life on earth — without photosynthesis there would be no oxygen, expelled by plants, for us to breathe.

Ptyalin A component of saliva. It breaks down food.

Sugar A word which in wine making contains a wealth of meanings, misunderstanding and sins. Sugar can be the sort which comes in bags, *soleil en sac* as the French have it, and is added, via the technique called chaptalization (after M. Chaptal, a Napoleonic minister), to much French wine. It would be better wine without it much of the time, but old habits die hard. Sugar as a natural product of the grape which yeast turns into alcohol is a more natural process. Sugar is present in all wine — a wine without any would be austere beyond relief. Sugar cannot be smelt yet it is, perhaps for this reason, the first thing the taste buds sense, since the taste-buds designed to alert us to sweetness are situated at the immediate tip of the tongue.

Tannin See Section in book on this crucial component of wine.

Terroir A French term referring to the combination of site, climate, disposition and soil of a particular vineyard or defined area of vines and the aggregate expression of these things as found in the wine(s). There is no exact English equivalent. This adds to the word's semi-mysticism. *Terroir* is now used internationally as a term conferring a measure of perceived (i.e. not necessarily actual) excellence on a wine; such a wine being said to 'express its *terroir*'. It can be a load of codswallop unless its fruit genuinely has an individuality recognizable as being a factor of *terroir* and not a figment of the wine producer's fantasies or the techniques of the wine's manufacture.

Tosspot A lovely word which comes down to us from the middle third of the sixteenth century meaning a person who 'tosses off his pot', that is say, someone who drinks a lot. Vulgar modern parlance has attempted to introduce some kind of sexual connotation to the word or to consider it interchangeable with wanker, for obvious reasons of comparable imagery, but this is incorrect. Many seasoned wine tasters are tosspots.

Trichloranisole See Chapter 13. 2-4-6 Trichloranisole is a chemical which affects a percentage of wine corks and passes a taint into the wine.

Vin de garde A wine, a posh bordeaux for example, which is not made for immediate drinking but produced for the cellar where it can mature and, it is hoped, reach its apogee of drinkability some years later. It is a popular term in wine class warfare, since any wine not a *vin de garde* is seen as inferior. This does not always bear any relationship to the real world. Many a New World cabernet of the previous year's vintage, for example, will taste more exciting than a red bordeaux aged for a decade, and be completely ready to drink A measure of the dubiety of the concept of the *vin de garde* is in the postponement of pleasure in which the customer willingly joins. Travelling hopefully has always been said to be more thrilling than to arrive and with old wine, when it is opened, this is often the case. But the exceptions exist, are marvellous (especially with certain sweet wines and rieslings), and so we drinkers continue to believe in the nirvana to come.

Volatile acidity (VA) A term (see Chapter 13) which is often used interchangeably with oxidation but is not precisely the same thing. Oxidation in a finished wine is the spoiling of the edge of the fruit by virtue of the wine having been exposed to air for too long. VA is strictly the more advanced form of this where air has reacted with alcohol to create volatile acids amongst which is acetic acid, or vinegar, and so the wine is said to be volatile — in a state where the vinegariness is detectable on the nose and palate. Bacterial action does the damage in wines with advanced volatility but it is important to realize that acetic acid is a by-product of fermentation in any case and it is present in tiny amounts in all wines. The balance of the other elements of a wine, the alcohol itself as well as the wine's fruitiness, other acids, and/or tannins, make any acetic acid merely a part of the wine's agreeable mix.

Volatile *sommelier* This is a situation which arises when a wine waiter refuses to recognize a fault in a wine and to replace it. Flying in the face of the common assumption that customers are in the restaurant to enjoy themselves, the volatile *sommelier* prefers torture. I have experience of a few such *sommeliers*, but I will not bore the reader with the matter further.

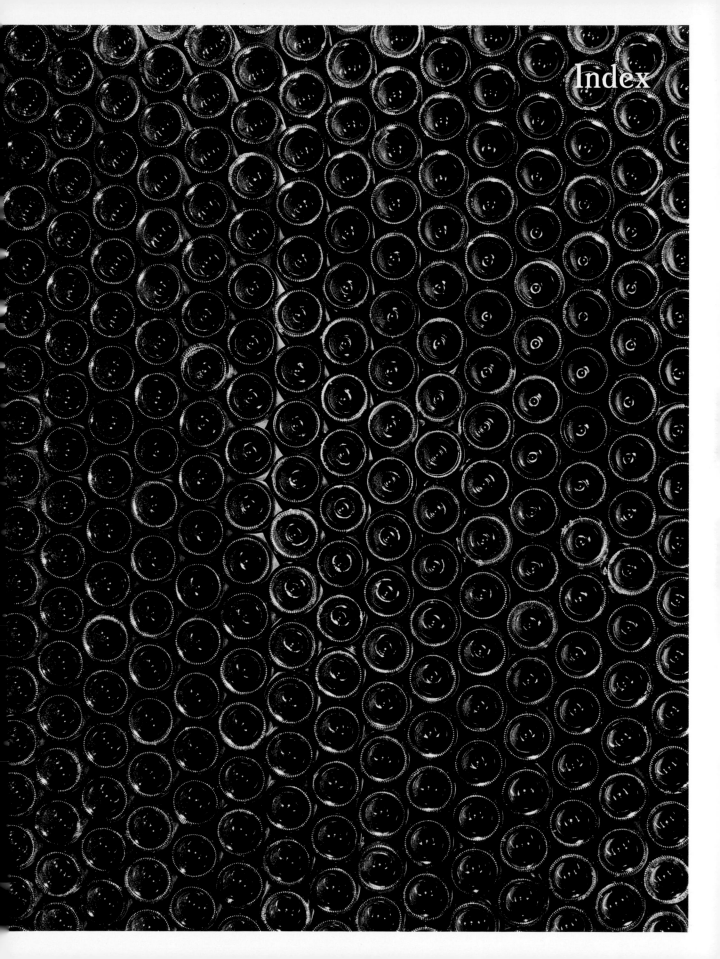

Index

Index

Figures in italics refer to captions.

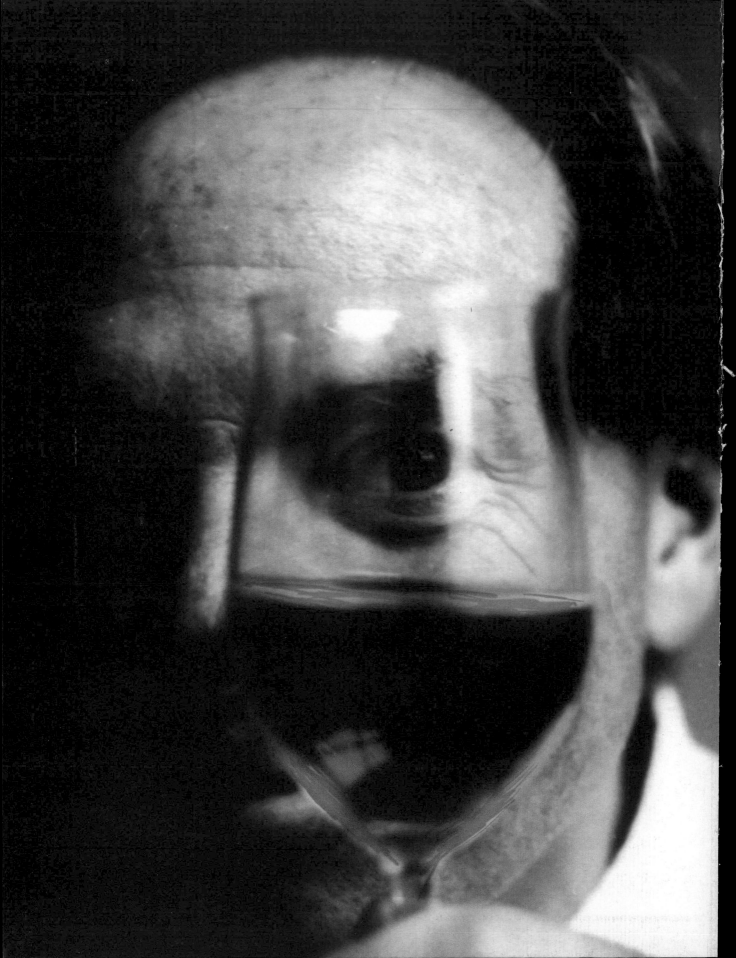